Endorsements

Once again Mark knocks it out of the park with a timely and incredibly necessary book filled with revelation. *Carriers of His Presence* is filled with course-altering wisdom aimed at igniting the heart of the believer into our authentic purpose and Abba's desire for us as His beloved priesthood. We were created to carry Presence. Mark carries such a unique gift in his writing, and every page swirls in the heart of the reader. I could not put this book down, and I am going to be making this required reading for the leadership of our church. I could not possibly recommend this book more as we shift from the dysfunctional religious and political spirit into a true kingdom expression; this book provides that road map.

Matt Brown, Pastor of The Homestead
Aubrey, Texas

This book has come at just the right time. Mark Casto has a now word from God that, if heeded, has the chance to shift God's church and its leaders for generations to come. Normal won't do. The church is at a crossroads. We must come back to Presence-led lives and leadership, and this book is a road map into the resurrection of that reality. This moment demands it! Jump in with your whole heart, and let us journey together as *Carriers of His Presence!*

Bryn A. Waddell, Pastor of City Revival Church
Kannapolis, North Carolina

It is now becoming clear that a growing number of believers, including leaders, are dissatisfied with man-made, stale, controlling, and anemic religious systems. This is especially true of the younger generation. The dissatisfaction has been planned/caused by God, who has placed in an entire generation an insatiable hunger for something they have yet to identify—but they're searching. At just the right moment, He will give them a taste of Himself, and the world will forever change. For this generation, like this era, is unlike any other. They are as untamable as they are unsatisfied, and will mark the planet with their unbridled love and passion for Christ.

If you are one of those hungering for more than organized religion, money, possessions, earthly pleasures, or even meaningful human relationships have been able to provide, *Carriers of His Presence* was written for you. You're about to be liberated from religious routine and passionless living and receive permission to pursue that which you've been longing for: the Presence and glory of God.

Dutch Sheets, Apostle

CARRIERS

of His

PRESENCE

MARK CASTO

CARRIERS
of His
PRESENCE

EXPOSING THE COMPROMISED PRIESTHOOD
AND POLITICAL SPIRIT BY RAISING UP
A PEOPLE OF HIS PRESENCE

DESTINY IMAGE® PUBLISHERS, INC.
P.O. Box 310, Shippensburg, PA 17257-0310
"Promoting Inspired Lives."

This book and all other Destiny Image and Destiny Image Fiction books are available at Christian bookstores and distributors worldwide.

For more information on foreign distributors, call 717-532-3040.

Reach us on the Internet: www.destinyimage.com.

ISBN 13 TP: 978-0-7684-6374-3

ISBN 13 eBook: 978-0-7684-6375-0

For Worldwide Distribution, Printed in the U.S.A.

1 2 3 4 5 6 7 8 / 26 25 24 23 22

Contents

Foreword

A movement is underway in the global church and that movement is now beginning to manifest in the Western part of the world.

What is the movement, you might ask? It is nothing short of a transformation in how we see God Himself. To embrace the Abba revealed in Jesus Christ rather than the austere, distant, disapproving god of Western religion is a revolutionary theological shift that is desperately needed in the church of our day. In order for this movement to gain its intended traction and become as pervasive as God longs for it to become, it will require a new breed of leader. Those leaders will need fathers—fathers cut from the fabric of the patristic and apostolic tradition rather than the post-modern expression of the leader longing for celebrity and social acknowledgment.

These fathers will play the essential role of permitting the next generation to be liberated from the trap of media-driven pseudo success and will enable rising leaders to rediscover a Kingdom definition of what it means to be truly and authentically successful. This success is solely measured by hosting and subsequently carrying the Presence of Jesus. These leaders will become the most significant voices of change and renewal on the earth in the decades to come, and I believe Mark Casto is becoming a first fruits of one of these rising voices.

I have had the distinct privilege of walking very closely with Mark and his precious family as they have made one courageous decision after another. He was uniquely positioned and groomed to be able to use his incredible gifting to succeed in the world of a "Christian celebrity" but chose the more excellent way. I say all of that to say Mark is the absolute right person to write this book and to extend this invitation to the church and her leaders. He has lived this journey and he has come to the glorious place in his heart where he can echo the cry of King David: "One thing have I desired of the Lord, that will I seek after, that I may dwell in the house of the Lord all the days of my life, to behold the beauty of the Lord and to inquire in His temple."

I recognize that some may struggle to receive this invitation, and I can certainly sympathize; however, to the handful of courageous ones who are willing to go against the flow of the current definition of "mainstream success," I can testify along with Mark, as well as so many others, that His Presence is the only thing that really matters. It's the only means whereby we will inherit the historic shift that is necessary if we are to carry Abba's love and power to the longing cosmos.

I've never been more filled with hope for the church, as I see these rising leaders step into their position, and this book is a blueprint to enable others to come out of the self-absorbed culture of the Western church and receive grace to yield to our invitation into abiding union with Father, Son, and Spirit. What you are holding is much more than a book—it's actually an invitation, and my prayer is for you to receive the grace that releases the courage to make the turn and take the journey. Trust me when I tell you, whatever you leave behind will not compare to the Presence you are being prepared to inherit.

Damon Thompson, Apostle
Mobile, Alabama

Introduction

A new reformation is upon us.

You don't have to be prophetic to sense the tension and need for transition in the church of the West. The people of God are waking up to what is possible while leaders are trying to maintain what's convenient.

The world is no longer blind to our hypocrisy and can see a noticeable difference between the church Jesus describes and the one we are currently projecting.

We are being exposed.

Ministers are falling, the next generation is leaving, and while we seek the statistics for why, the answers cannot be found through a carnal lens. We have to admit that we have trained people to call our man-made hype "the church" while not tending to the most essential aspect that makes us who we are—the Presence of Jesus in our midst.

We need a leader shift.

A transition from the position-obsessed political kingdom of Saul to the Presence-obsessed heart of a David. Can we not see that the world is not impressed with our titles or positions, degrees and facilities, not to mention the people we enslave by our narcissistic and political view of leadership?

Can we acknowledge that the world is not better even though the church has become more gifted? Would we even dare to admit that our ambitious gatherings led by personality-driven ministries have not made a lasting impact upon the culture?

The church has actually become somewhat popular in the past forty years owning our own satellites, television and radio stations, and we are featured on media platforms worldwide. But I think we can see now that no amount of position, money, influence, or strategy can satisfy a world hungry for the tangible, supernatural Presence of God. If we are to see His Kingdom come and His will be done on earth as it is in heaven, then we must own what we have become, admit our mistakes, and humbly embrace a more excellent way.

When man fell in the garden, Yahweh asked Adam, "Where are you?" Not because He did not know where Adam's physical being was located, but rather to see if Adam knew where he was. Today, I can hear the Father's voice calling to us, saying, "America, where are you? Where is the nation that I want to display as a city set upon a hill that cannot be hidden?"

However, before a nation can answer that question, those of us who are in the body of Christ must respond first. Where are His Davids? Men and women who are Presence-obsessed image-bearers willing to play our harps faithfully in the field for the audience of One? Where are those who would remain faithful to Jesus even while dwelling in the caves of obscurity? This is the posture of a man Yahweh said is after His own heart.

Can you sense we are in the days of transition, much like the days between the house of Saul and the house of David? Yet God was faithful to deliver the nation from a political king to find one in whom He could enthrone Himself upon the altar of his heart. That one man who made the Presence of God a big deal in his own life became the man who restored the Presence of God to his city, brought peace to a nation, and unlocked opulent wealth for the next generation.

Let the leader shift begin.

Yahweh is calling for change. May we respond by answering the call to come out of all other temporal obsessions to become the image bearers who are obsessed with One Thing—the Presence of the One who rescued us, Jesus!

Today, we find ourselves in the same leadership parallels of ancient Israel in the days leading to David's reign as king. Israel went from a powerful nation inheriting its Promised Land and being miraculously delivered by God's divine providence to a nation desperately in need of God's Presence.

We, like Israel, are left desperate for God's Presence after years of being led by a compromised priesthood living only to serve themselves, prophets who would rather travel the circuit than raise sons, and by political kings who would rather enslave every-one to their vision instead of equipping people to display the authentic image of Christ in the earth.

We need to shift away from the entertainment culture of American Christianity being led by ambitious business leaders with no fear of the Lord.

We need to shift away from the prophetic movement that values being featured on conference platforms on the road more than being planted at home to ensure we raise up the next generation.

We must shift away from the political kings who build monuments to themselves while enslaving the people of God to their idea of ministerial success.

The compromise among present leaders in the American church has caused people to despise serving the Lord. Have you noticed a generation crying from their social platforms about modern-day spiritual abuse and taking deep dives into the post-modern thinking of "deconstruction?" They aren't rebellious; they are confused, hurting, and broken. They no longer see church leaders as models of integrity, so they leave because no one will sit still long enough to raise them up into the fullness of their unique design.

But the Davids are coming.

A Presence-obsessed leader who no longer values what's best for themselves, but knows there is no greater pursuit of a king than to restore what made Israel great and that was the Presence of Yahweh in their midst.

A Presence-obsessed leader who doesn't get caught in the trappings of religion, politics, or ministerial success, but says let's make it all evolve around Him!

I write this book for you, the seekers—men and women who will become the leaders desperate to leave behind the failing models of the Western religious system and build a new culture that evolves around the simplicity of life lived obsessed with the Presence of the Lord.

Will you take this journey with me? To come face to face with the problematic parallels of ancient Israel and into a whole new way of thinking? If you have read this far, don't stop here. Abba is leading us back to His original intent, and it will certainly be needed for the days ahead.

This is a message for the exiles, the misfits who no longer feel comfortable in the compromised Western church—you are being called home, back to the order of fathers and sons where you can be enfolded into the family of God as the sons of glory!

The Compromised Priesthood

You don't lose the Presence of God overnight.

It is usually a long process of consistent disobedience to Yahweh's plan.

So it was in the days of ancient Israel. Following the days of Joshua's great conquest, with Israel firmly planted in their promised land, they were in a constant cycle of idolatry, adversaries, repentance, and deliverance.

Israel was living in a time much like our nation today when "everyone did what seemed right to them" (Judges 21:25 VOICE). Yet, in the book of 1 Samuel, we find that it wasn't just the people who were doing what they thought was right—they were being led by a compromised priesthood who did whatever they wanted.

This compromised priesthood consisted of a father, Eli, and his two corrupt sons, Hophni and Phinehas. Eli served for 40 years as a judge for Israel and a priest in Shiloh. He was fat, nearly blind, and while he enjoyed the position he had, he could not discern the desperation and birthing of a new thing in Israel. The Bible speaks clearly to the failings of Eli as a father, naming his sons "worthless men" (1 Sam. 2:12 ESV). It was Eli who, through failing as a father, began this cycle of destructive leadership in Israel by not correcting his sons and cleaning out the house of the Lord.

The sons of Eli were considered morally corrupt and worthless men. They did not know the Lord and didn't walk in the lifestyle expected of a priest. They oozed with the sin of ambition and greed. They made up their own rules in a time when their priestly duties were laid out plainly. If that wasn't enough, these men operated in sexual perversion, sleeping with the women who served at the entrance of the tent of meeting, leading the nation into perversion and greed.

Today we see the spirits of Hophni and Phinehas alive in this compromised priesthood that has infiltrated the Western church through the guise of gifts and talents, titles, and positions. We have all read the stories of senior pastors sleeping with students in their youth ministries, church leaders committing adultery with their assistants, and charismatic celebrity church leaders sleeping with their "fans" and offering them the morning-after pill. Where is the fear of the Lord?

Unfortunately, it's easy to find the root of this rebellion. After decades of scandals, especially among the Pentecostal/Charismatic world, we have become numb to the almost daily stories of ministers being exposed in compromised choices and lifestyles. We have allowed men to take positions without the fruit of devotion to Jesus.

Because we have dishonored the gift of the apostle in our day, we are dealing with a fatherless epidemic among church leaders. The fear of the Lord has been replaced with greed and ambition. Because we lost the love of His Presence, we lost our ultimate source of contentment and began to pursue money instead of Him.

Hebrews 13:5 warns us, "Keep your lives free from the love of money and be content with what you have, because God has said, 'Never will I leave you; never will I forsake you'" (NIV). Our greatest inheritance is not the wealth received. The Presence of the One who promised to never forsake us stands with us to provide for our each and every step of the way.

Because we have so few fathers in the American church, many church leaders have become a law unto themselves. They never learned the experiential knowledge of God gained in intimacy, understood the fear of the Lord, or learned to live vulnerably or allow someone to hold them accountable to the standards of New Testament leadership.

Today, we see both men and women in church leadership oozing with ambition who have traded their intimacy with God for business strategies. We have lost the knowledge of God for a complete indoctrination of Babylon. Church leadership was expected to carry on orthodoxy, study theology, and know God intimately. Today you are more likely to find their libraries full of business and marketing books to leverage their influence and gain self-help productivity hacks.

The Kingdom of God's idea of significance was traded for Babylon's idea of success. When that happened, we lost the fear of the Lord, and people became nothing more than numbers and tithe checks.

The compromised priesthood says, "How can we leverage our position and titles for personal gain or sexual pleasure?" Again, this didn't happen overnight. It started with unsubmitted leaders functioning in small acts of compromise over an extended period of time.

Entertainment standards have caused us to value positions, titles, gifts, and talents more than inspecting the fruit of a leader's character. As long as church leaders played their role on the platform and put on a good show for us once a week, we ignored their compromise.

Yet, if Eli had truly confronted his sons' sins as a father, this vicious cycle of destructive leadership and subsequent loss of the Presence of God could have been thwarted. God spoke to Eli saying, "You have honored your sons more than me, by making yourselves fat with the best part of all of the offerings of my people Israel" (1 Sam. 2:29 CSB).

The Presence of God was lost in a nation. Not primarily because of the sons' sins, but the unwillingness of a father to confront and correct his sons. Sadly, we know that Eli did not fully deal with his sons because he benefited from their compromise.

Eli not only grew fat from their greed, but God also said that he honored his sons more than Him. Maybe we don't realize it, but the compromised priesthood honors what we helped create more than we honor Yahweh.

We must be careful not to create, build, or value something above the ways of God especially when Yahweh is asking for us to make Him the center of it all!

How often do we see the Presence of God being shoved out of the room so that our vision can be displayed? Today's act of adultery among the priesthood is far greater than Hophni and

Phinehas because we ask the Bride of Christ to take their gaze off of the Groom and onto ourselves.

Pastors who once led the flock are now leading their groupies, fans, and partners to worship their gift instead of the Presence of the One who called us. We see "kingdoms" being built in the name of personalities, not realizing the Presence of God is no longer being honored in His own house.

We need fathers today to warn their sons, as the apostle Paul did to his spiritual son Timothy in 1 Timothy 6:9, that "those who desire to be rich fall into temptation, into a snare, into many senseless and harmful desires that plunge people into ruin and destruction" (ESV). He continues by saying, "Some people, eager for money, have wandered from the faith and pierced themselves with many griefs" (1 Tim. 6:10 NIV).

Please listen. Money, buildings, and good causes are not the real issue. The primary pursuit of it distracts and eventually leads to the absence of devotion to Jesus. Leaders now treat ministry like business contracts. They don't pray about where they should be, but they look for the more advantageous opportunity for personal gain.

Young men leave seminary prepared to start an enterprise and are ill-equipped theologically for the ministry. Pastors are spending more time recruiting and fleecing their flocks with the latest multi-level marketing schemes instead of teaching them that God gives us the power to create wealth (see Deut. 8:18). Offerings are more about the vision of the church than true honor for the Lord.

For years we have blamed the nation's condition on sinners, yet how will a city or country know how to live if they have no example? Maybe we should put down our rocks of religion that we aim at the world and realize it is always the compromise of the priesthood that leads to the perversion of a nation.

Nations are no different today. As the body of Christ, we are now the ambassadors who are to represent the Kingdom of God to the world. We are to be image-bearers, kings, and priests unto God, carriers of His Presence standing before a culture desperate for His Presence, true identity, and purpose. If we fail to acknowledge His Presence, we lose our most valuable possession that makes cultural transformation possible.

This is how Israel lost His Presence. When Israel needed Yahweh the most, the compromised priesthood led the people into a battle they could not win without His Presence being the priority. What was the cost in their day? Thirty thousand men, the elimination of the priesthood, and their most prized possession, the Ark of His Presence, in the hands of their enemies.

The Traveling Prophet

The compromised priesthood ushered in a new day for Israel. "In those days the word of the Lord was rare and prophetic visions were not widespread" (1 Sam. 3:1 CSB). Eli's eyesight was failing and the lamp of God was growing dim in the temple, and in the middle of the cesspool of religion, Yahweh was raising up a prophet.

The answer for a compromised priesthood is a faithful priest.

> Then I will raise up a faithful priest for myself. He will do whatever is in my heart and mind. I will establish a lasting dynasty for him, and he will walk before my anointed one for all time (1 Samuel 2:35 CSB).

Before Samuel ever became one of the greatest prophets in the history of Israel, it began with being a faithful priest before the Lord.

His accolades are beyond my ability to fit them into this section of the book. However, we must recognize the significance of this man. "Samuel grew, and the Lord was with him and let none of his words fall to the ground" (1 Sam. 3:19 ESV).

Samuel called Israel to return to the Lord with all of their heart, helped eradicate idolatry from the land, and led them in times of prayer and fasting. Because of Samuel, the Lord's hand protected Israel from the Philistines and they were able to recover forfeited lands.

His faithfulness was proved by the reliability Israel had in his messages from Yahweh. All of Israel soon recognized he was a prophet of the Lord and the new judge of the nation. Israel had found their answer in a traveling prophet.

> *Every year he would go on a circuit to Bethel, Gilgal, and Mizpah and would judge Israel at all these locations. Then he would return to Ramah because his home was there, he judged Israel there, and he built an altar to the Lord there* (1 Samuel 7:16-17 CSB).

While we indeed celebrate the extraordinary life of Samuel, many refuse to speak of his mistakes. Chapters of the Bible are dedicated to his incredible life of public ministry, but it's not until Israel cries out for a king like other nations that we discover that Samuel even had sons.

His wife and sons are never mentioned within the pages of scripture that speak of his powerful ministry. When we do hear of his family, Israel rejects his sons as judges over them because he failed to raise them in his ways.

His sons, Joel and Abijah, turned toward dishonest profit, took bribes, and perverted justice. How could it be that one of the greatest prophets to walk the land of Israel could have sons not walking in his ways?

Because when prophets are not home, they fail to raise up sons.

From my own experience of being an itinerant evangelist, traveling the country, and meeting those who were able to do it full time, we were all taught that you had to sacrifice family on the altar of ministry. Unfortunately, I believe Samuel chose the circuit over his sons.

Although Samuel served faithfully as a priest, prophet, and judge, he failed as a father, and when the nation needed leaders they realized that it takes more than a father's chromosomes to raise sons.

Please don't think I fail to see that historically God has used broken men to accomplish His will. However, I don't believe that is permission not to learn from their mistakes.

We are making this same mistake today. The church is living codependent upon the "traveling prophets" at the expense of their own families. We celebrate outstanding spiritual accomplishments in public ministry but fail to see these men and women raise natural or even spiritual offspring.

This word about traveling prophets is a very personal subject for me because I was on the path of sacrificing my family for the cause. Being a father of three at the time, and yet traveling forty-two weekends out of the year while pastoring a church doesn't give much opportunity to be the father Yahweh has called you to be.

Sadly, I know ministry children who barely knew their fathers or grandfathers all because that was the price they were taught to pay for the sake of the Kingdom.

An example for our day would be the extraordinary ministry of Billy Graham. We celebrate him for decades of reaching the world with the message of the gospel, but very few know of the devastation that his absence caused in his home.

Shortly after Graham's passing, *The Washington Post* wrote an article on Graham as a father and his relationship with his children:

> When their first child, Virginia, was born in 1945, Billy was away on a preaching trip. As Graham's crusades took him throughout the world, little was left for Ruth and the children. …Once, when Ruth brought Anne to a crusade and let her surprise her father while he was talking on the telephone, he stared at the toddler with a blank look, not recognizing his own daughter. In a turnabout a few years later, young Franklin greeted his father's homecoming from a crusade with a puzzled "Who's he?"[1]

I don't share this story to dishonor Billy Graham, but only to expose you to the devastation of the traveling prophet. Unfortunately, this small story in the life of the most famous evangelist in modern times led to deeper wounds and problems for his family and children. A failing model of ministry teaches us to reach the world and neglect our primary responsibility to raise up the next generation.

When it came time for Samuel to bear the fruit of generational legacy, expanding his influence beyond his years, he had nothing to show. Yes, there were incredible stories of miracles, thunder, and victory over the Philistines. But while the people rejoiced for the miracles and thunder, what no one could hear was a cry from two sons for a present father.

It was time for transition in Israel, and not only had the compromised priesthood lost the Presence of God, but the traveling prophet also failed to raise sons who could lead the nation.

Lessons like Samuel and his two sons remind us that family is the bedrock of all society, and some of our most anointed leaders are failing this same test. We need fathers like Paul, who told his spiritual son Timothy:

> *If any of you aspires to be an overseer in the church… His heart should be set on guiding his household with wisdom and dignity; bringing up his children to worship with devotion and purity. For if he's unable to properly lead his own household well, how could he properly lead God's household?* (1 Timothy 3:1,4-5)

Paul went on to say to the church in Corinth that if you want to give yourself entirely to the ministry alone, then remain single. We can't afford to continually repeat the vicious cycle. Once you are married and have the incredible privilege to raise children, your family has become your primary ministry in the eyes of God. You cannot be married and give to Abba the same ministry commitment as those who are single.

The traveling prophet life seems glamorous—laying hands on the multitudes and being applauded for your gift. Still, in the eyes of Yahweh, He honors the day-in and the day-out of preparing a generational legacy that lives beyond your years of ministry.

Will we continue Samuel's path? Will we be satisfied with the applause of man for public victories while failing in secret with our family? Or will we learn to rest in the reality of creating a Kingdom legacy within our own home?

What could Samuel's sons have done in the nation of Israel had dad been involved in their lives at home? I'm not sure many of us even know their names, but how could we? Their legacy died with their father. May we not repeat this curse. I refuse to rescue a generation and lose my children. I refuse to be another father addicted to the ministry with great stories to tell at my funeral but no sons who can take my place. Will you make the same stand with me?

May we all agree that ministry and busyness will no longer be a cause for fatherlessness within the Kingdom. I declare ministry will no longer usher the orphan spirit right into the children of church leaders. This same principle applies to business leaders and entrepreneurs—don't waste your life on personal destiny. Make sure the next generation knows you love being present in their lives; it may be the only way Presence is restored to our nation.

Be the priest of your home, look your wife and children in the eyes, and make sure you're not winning the world and losing them.

This cycle of dysfunctional leadership continued to grow in Israel. Because the traveling prophet valued personal destiny over generational legacy, he had to anoint a political king. A nation that once depended upon its prophets would soon depend on politics.

The Political King

Israel's dependence upon the powerful public ministry of Samuel prepared them to beg for a political king like other nations. Saul was a man who stood out as the natural choice, with his head and shoulders taller than everyone.

Although his beginnings were promising and full of supernatural activity, the political spirit did not take long to take root within his heart. Samuel had already warned the people present for Saul's coronation that he was clearing his hands of any wrongdoing, reminding them of God's dealings with their ancestors and that God was once their King.

Yet God granted them their request—one man to rule over them. I cannot imagine how Saul felt as Samuel chastised the people during his coronation. He called their desire for a king wickedness.

He went on to explain the behavior of a king. Their sons would no longer be free to follow their occupation but would instead be reduced to servants as the king saw fit. Some would be taken from their own fields to plow and reap the king's fields, while others would be used to make weapons of war. Even the daughters of Israel would be taken to perform the jobs of perfumers, cooks, and bakers. Because the traveling prophet failed to raise sons, it gave way for a political king to enslave sons.

A political king would take the best of their fields, vineyards, and olive groves and give them to his servants. Do you recognize what just happened to them when they chose a king? Immediately, sons were reduced to slaves, inheritances were lost, and the best lands with their crops could be taken from them.

Israel was ready to forfeit its inheritance for an immediate false security in the name of political assurance. Samuel warned them that the tax and toll would make them cry out to God, but they would not be heard.

In 1 and 2 Kings, Samuel warned them that they could come under judgment for their king's actions. If the king did right in the sight of the Lord, Israel was blessed. If the king did evil in the sight of the Lord, Israel was cursed.

These people were willing to risk their relationship and favor with God to have someone rule over them. The price they would pay would be much more than they anticipated. Unfortunately for Israel, Saul would serve for decades but only carry the anointing for the kingdom his first two years.

The traveling prophet and the political king would bump heads many times during this transition of dysfunctional leadership. Saul thought he was above the Law of God and took matters into his own hands, even defying Samuel and the word of the Lord. What kind of price do servants pay to follow political kings? In one instance, on the day of battle, the only two people equipped for war were King Saul and his son, Jonathan.

This selfish behavior exists among some leaders today. Some could not care less about the equipping of the saints because they entered into church leadership for personal gain. Today, many church leaders are under the same influence of the spirit of Saul, reducing God's sons and daughters to slaves, taking the best of their resources, talents, and time and enslaving them to their own vision. This was never God's intention for the church.

One of Saul's first commands from the Lord was the task of destroying God's enemies, the Amalekites. The order from the prophet Samuel was to destroy everything, leaving nothing. Saul obeyed the Lord except he spared the Amalekite king, the best of the sheep and goats, and anything that appealed to him.

Political kings will obey God as long as it appeals to what seems good to them. Today, many in the church find themselves enslaved to these types of leaders, who do what appeals to their vision, caring little for the direction of the word of the Lord.

Even in light of his disobedience, Saul went from there to build a monument of himself. This explains why he kept all that looked good from his battle with the Amalekites. Saul saw everything through the eyes of what could make him look good in front of the people. This will become the bottom line for any political leader. Even though they put on the façade that they are strong, brick by brick they build monuments out of their bondage to the fear of man.

It is the fear of man that makes political kings like Saul such dangerous leaders. Because they fear the people, they are willing to do anything to keep their position, even if it means running off those God has actually chosen to lead His people into a new day.

Political kings thrive on the applause of man and use personal monuments as cover-ups for disobedience. If they can impress you with what they build, maybe you will forget their compromise. This is why political leaders and systems will never be able to restore God's Presence back to our lives—because they demand to be the center of attention.

Once Saul realized his sin, things got worse. This mighty leader's true colors began to shine, exposing the fact that he indeed was nothing more than a political figure filled with pride.

When Samuel confronted Saul with his disobedience, his excuse was that he feared the people and listened to their voices. Anyone in their right mind would have met this rebuke with humility, but instead he asked Samuel to honor him before the people so no one would think he did anything wrong.

This was nothing more than propaganda—a stage full of actors to keep the people he just blamed for his actions enslaved to his leadership. This type of insecurity and pride is in full force today among many leaders within the church, building personality cults instead of establishing a culture where people can encounter the Presence of the Lord.

These types of political kings can keep an entire generation, including our prophets, from encountering the Lord. In Isaiah 6:1-4, we could all quote, "In the year that King Uzziah died, I saw the Lord." But have we ever explored the depths of how important this statement was?

Uzziah was anointed as king of Judah at just 16 years of age. As long as Uzziah sought the Lord, God prospered him. He was incredibly intelligent and innovative, carrying Israel into victory over both the Philistines and Arabs. He brought stability and protection to Judah by building fortified towers and strengthened the armies of Judah.

Eventually, King Uzziah's fame spread everywhere. One day the king decided to go into the temple and offer incense before God, which was against the law for a king to do. This act of pride was Uzziah declaring that he was above the proper protocol of God. He even railed against the priest who rebuked him, causing leprosy to break out on his head.

He kept the position of king, but was never allowed in the Presence of God again. Just because you are anointed, doesn't mean you get to do whatever you want. Leaders who feel this way and feel they are above authority eventually fall into a lifestyle of sin.

But when King Uzziah died, Isaiah saw the Lord. Uzziah's fame caused God's glory to be hidden behind his renown.

We need to deal with this political spirit inside of us. The desire to be seen, the ambition to be known, the desire to obtain more—whatever it is, we must deal with this political spirit because it is keeping people from seeing Jesus!

A Word of Caution to the Prophetic Movement

While it is true that traveling prophets many times fail to raise sons, Samuel was given a moment when he could correct his mistake and replace a political king with God's chosen one. Yet on the day of transition, Samuel made another critical error that we will make today if we are not careful.

The only reason why a political king like Saul was able to maintain his position in Israel without the anointing to lead it was that, following his disobedience, Samuel went on Saul's platform to worship and wave to the people like he had done nothing wrong.

I remember sitting in a meeting with my spiritual father, Damon Thompson. Several other sons were present when he looked at us and said, "Don't allow your anointing to be used to prop up a system that Yahweh is trying to replace."

When traveling prophets are willing to play the role of an actor on the stage of politics, we continue the cycle of dysfunctional leadership. The spirit of Saul wants you to stand on his platform and use your anointing so that people will think his platform is still relevant. He wants to use the revelation intended for David to help him remain as king.

I know this can be difficult at times because many in the prophetic community have to watch people whom they anointed, helped get started, and commissioned, only to see them fall within the church. But it's one thing to restore a man, and it's an entirely different thing to cover it up as if nothing happened.

I will tell you why I believe it's difficult for many in this day of transition. It is because currently those who operate in the political spirit of Saul still have big platforms, influence, and resources. Again, I'm not saying we should not seek to restore them in private, but there is undoubtedly a time when you should not stand on their platform in public until you know there is complete restoration in private.

For many, to confront someone in their failure and refuse to stand with them in public until there is complete restoration in private, would be too costly of a price. You not only have to walk away from Saul, but you have to be willing to disconnect from his platform, the crowds, and his resources. You might have helped get them started, but it is not dishonoring to disconnect.

You will actually dishonor them if you stay.

So my question to the Samuels of today is, "How long will you mourn for Saul?" How long will you continue to prop up the political church systems with crowds and resources but have no anointing to bring true cultural transformation? How long will you continue waving at the people when you know God is longing to bring forth a new type of leader?

If you are still standing on the platform of Saul, Israel will never find their Davids. These leaders—whom the spirit of Saul hated, who have been pushed out and ostracized—are waiting for you to find them playing their harps faithfully for an audience of One.

Who will leave the kingdom of Saul and his platform to find the Davids who carry Presence? It will take a real encounter with God and the absence of ambition to leave an established system, where you can wave at crowds, to find the Davids in tiny houses.

There Is a Leader Shift Coming

While the nation of Israel was a complete mess, it was from this background of a compromised priesthood, a traveling prophet, and a political king that a new kind of leader was born. While we may find ourselves in similar parallels in the Western church, we should not lose hope.

A young shepherd boy with a harp in his hand is being groomed to become the shepherd of a nation. He will slay giants one day, but today he is learning to kill the lions and bears. He will have to learn to overcome family rejection, dodge the spears of Saul, and live among the caves. But it's to ensure that the cycle of dysfunctional leadership finally gives way, not to a perfect man, but a man obsessed with the Presence of God.

These Davids will not be trained for the priesthood, raised in the school of the prophets, nor will they carry the bloodline of great religious pedigrees. They are being chosen because of their hunger for one thing! *Him.*

Samuel, your mourning days are over. Instead of rebuking, correcting, and fixing what God is trying to replace—go find David.

When the Anointed Stand in the Way of the Glory

Biggest warning to those operating in the spirit of Saul—know when to move out of the way, because this generation is making the transition into the glory realm.

In 2013, Apostle Damon Thompson began declaring that we are making a transition from the anointing to the glory. When I first heard him declare this word I felt the Spirit of the Lord speak to me that if we are not careful, those who will pay the highest price in the days of the Spirit's move will be those anointed to lead it.

The spirit of Saul is alive and well among leadership today. It is not alive and well in the hearts of leaders because of their own choices alone—we have positioned them in this dangerous place. Because of their anointing, gifts, and abilities, many have chosen, as the children of Israel in Moses' day, to live codependent upon the leader's relationship with God.

What a dangerous combination when codependent followers exalt insecure leaders filled with the political spirit of Saul. When these two mingle together, they produce the same results as the fall of lucifer.

Lucifer was the anointed cherub who was over the protocol of worship in heaven. He was anointed to reveal the glory of God. But when pride seeks to remain the featured attraction, those called to reveal Him become those who conceal Him from others. We cannot make this same mistake and start admiring our own beauty in the anointing, loving the recognition, and allowing our hearts to be lifted up.

Lucifer used his anointing, which brings people into the Presence of God, to lead them to behold him instead of the glory of Yahweh. But nothing will separate God from the people He is trying to reveal Himself to—even those who were originally anointed to do so.

The day of the Moses show is over! No more of having one man go into the Presence of God and pull the curtain back for us once a week when we need them to perform and then close the curtain when we are done so that we don't have to look at what we have access to—at what we ourselves could become.

Did Moses have a part to play? Of course, God gave Moses specific instructions concerning how to build the tabernacle. "So Moses finished the work. Then the cloud covered the tabernacle of meeting" (Exod. 40:33-34 NKJV). While we honor Moses for leading the way, God never intended for Moses to become the pinnacle of Judaism. It was to be His glory.

This has become a problem in our generation. While we should always show honor and show double honor to those who lead us in the things of God, we lift people up to a place they do not belong. God's intention wasn't to simply watch men like a spectator sport, but for us all to see Him through these men.

We must move beyond the spectator message of beholding and step into the New Testament message of becoming.

John the Baptist was a voice anointed to prepare the way of the Lord and prepare a people for the Lord. Jesus said of him, "He was a burning and shining lamp, and you were willing to rejoice for a while in his light" (John 5:35 ESV).

His message was to repent and behold the Lamb of God. Those are two amazing and much-needed messages. But those aren't messages to fill altars and keep people coming back to our gatherings. Those words should give way to becoming.

People repented and were baptized, but when the glory of God was revealed many remained beholders only. Beholders are spectator Christians who come and watch anointed ministry but they never become anything.

Beholders live by the Old Testament model of ministry. One man goes into the Presence for us, tends the lampstand, and brings out the fresh bread and we live off their anointing. Many today are outer-court Christians who, at best, manage sin cycles because we have never moved beyond beholding to become something.

Jesus has ripped the veil of the Old Covenant mindset and calls us into His face, where we don't just behold—we become Him! While we are extremely thankful for John's voice, he knew when to get out of the way. His message of beholding the Lamb has to give way to "Come follow Me and I will make you fishers of men."

Let me give you some definitions for *anointing*, *Presence*, and *glory* so this will make sense. Each of these definitions comes from the message that Apostle Damon shared in 2013.

The anointing is empowerment given to release heaven's dimension. Heaven's dimension is what we call the Presence of God.

The Presence of God is the tangible expression that God is present in a space in time among His people.

The anointing is released to make us aware of the Presence of God. Once the Presence of God is acknowledged, we can move beyond the gifts and anointings of individuals and begin to engage the Presence of God.

It is what we do as a people with the Presence of God that determines whether we return to relying on the anointings of others or we move into the next dimension called glory.

What is glory? The transformative dimension of God in the earth where God's preeminence is manifest among men.

If leaders carry the spirit of Saul, it will be impossible for people codependent upon their leadership to experience the glory of the Lord. Humility is required in order for the Presence of God to take preeminence among men. You will have to learn as leaders that our call is to stay under the weight of His Presence, not stand in front of Him. We must move out of the way when He is ready to take over.

I remember being in a service that same year of this word being released. I had just finished preaching and the altars were completely full; not a single person remained in their seat. As normal, I was walking back and forth on the platform praying over the people. It was a very weighty moment in the Presence of God.

I heard the voice of the Lord say, "Go hide behind the speakers." It came with the full force of the fear of the Lord. I felt convicted to stand before the people in that moment and obeyed. I literally dove behind two large subwoofer speakers stacked on top of each other. As I lay there I heard Him speak again: "Mark, I don't mind you being My voice, but your voice cannot replace My face."

In these days of the Western church being led by the political leadership of Saul, we have let people's voices replace His face, and it is a dangerous place to be.

It reminds me of a story I heard from an older gentleman who played the organ for many years for many of the well-known tent evangelists in the healing revival. He told me about William Branham visiting H. Richard Hall in Cleveland, Tennessee, to have a conversation.

William Branham was at the height of his ministry—thousands were being healed and miracles were manifesting continuously. Yet he said to H. Richard Hall, "The Lord is about to take me home." And Brother Hall said, "Why would God do that? Your ministry is touching the world." William Branham replied, "The people are beginning to worship me instead of God."

Three weeks later William Branham died in a car accident. While this is a tragedy, it gives us a very great warning. Because of our heavy dependence on anointed ministry, a generation has lost many great men and women. Worse, we have lost the intentional pursuit of a life of devotion to Jesus that results in glory invading our lives. We have settled for spectator Christianity, where personal intimacy gets replaced with Christian entertainment that many call "worship" so that they will come back to our churches.

Then many wonder, once the freshness of the entertainment wanes, where is the supernatural Presence of God? He remains veiled until we leave the Moses show and those who are anointed to lead finally move out of the way.

We must repent for becoming spectators of anointed ministry, and anointed ministry must have enough humility to reject any Saul-like tendencies and know when it's time to move out of the way.

We need more men like John the Baptist, who was born in the house of priests and could have potentially become the next High Priest, but instead he rejected his father's broken system of religion and went to the wilderness.

In the wilderness he learned that he was a voice to prepare the way of the Lord and to make room for God. Although many thought he was the Messiah because of the noticeable influence he was attracting, he spoke clearly, "It is He who, coming after me, is preferred before me" (John 1:27 NKJV).

When he was able to release the message of "Behold the Lamb of God," his disciples began to follow Jesus. The religious leaders began to ask him how he felt about that. John's reply is the answer for all who are anointed to lead: "I'm friends with the Bridegroom. I rejoice greatly, and was glad to do my part. He must increase, but I must decrease" (see John 3:27-30).

Are we able to respond this way? The Lord is looking for leaders who are glad to do their part in this move of the Spirit many are calling the Presence movement. If so, you won't be able to participate with those who have made the ministry into an industry.

Jesus is not an entrepreneur building a business. He is a Bridegroom after a Bride and He is jealous for her. He is watching to see who His friends are. It's personal to Him how we treat her.

Will we preach Jesus only to proclaim ourselves to her? She will certainly notice our anointing, but remember our anointing is not to steal her gaze—it's to make sure she has a clear view of Him! We must be friends of the Bridegroom.

Unfortunately for Israel, they had a leader who didn't know how to move out of the way and they all paid an extraordinary price. It would cost Saul his life and the life of his son in the same place where Israel lost the Presence of God under the leadership of the compromised priesthood.

We need *Presence-obsessed leadership.*

Moses had a promise that he would take the children of Israel into the Promised Land; however, he was a Presence-obsessed man. In Exodus 33, Moses made it clear that the Promised Land meant nothing if the Presence of Yahweh did not go with them.

We need people who value Yahweh's Presence over any promise, vision, or mission. These are the leaders God seeks to raise up in our day. Ones who know that there is nothing special about us or a promise if it's absent of the Presence of Jesus!

I know we would much rather see a transfer of leadership like Elijah to Elisha or Moses to Joshua, but the political pursuit of "ministry" that has been modeled for decades in the Western church will most likely force a transition much like the kingdom of Saul to the kingdom of David.

But don't lose hope—we must be patient because the Bible says that there was a long war between the house of Saul and the house of David. It might take some time. Nevertheless, the Davids are coming.

My friend Bobby Lemley received a word from Abba in September of 2016 that I want to share with you:

> Remember once, when there was a clamor to find Saul to lead the nation, I was perfecting the heart of David, My Beloved, who was just hanging out with Me on the hillside. There is such a need for revival in the nation today, but it's not only going to come through political reform; it's going to come when a small segment of people have found their place in the silence of the hillside, learning to be an unshakeable son. Deliverance for a nation doesn't come just because the "right" person is in office; it's because unshakeable sons like David (Beloved) came off the hillside and said, "I have history with Yahweh."

It's time to shift our focus because the Lord is moving on from the personality-driven ministry paradigms to find Presence-obsessed leaders who will place His Presence back at the center of it all.

For those who are considering the path before them, A.W. Tozer gives us some perspective for a generation that no longer trusts political church leadership and is desperate to discover the Presence of God when he says:

> The whole Bible and all the great saints of the past join to tell us the same thing. "Take nothing for granted," they say to us. "Go back to the grass roots. Open your hearts and search the Scriptures. Bear your cross, follow your Lord and pay no heed to the passing religious vogue. The masses are always wrong. In every

generation the number of the righteous is small. Be sure you are among them."[2]

David and his men were but a small remnant in Israel, and considering the background from which they emerged, it's no wonder he asked one question that would change his entire nation. It's a question the compromised priesthood, traveling prophet, and political king should have asked, but they didn't.

What was the question that David asked that would change the history of Israel?

"How can the Ark of the Lord ever come to me?"

David's Journey to Restoring the Presence of God

"These things are written for an example."

Looking at Israel and its history with God can help us understand where we are today. Although written thousands of years ago, scripture is very much alive, divinely inspired, and we can find ourselves in every story.

When we read of Abraham's invitation to leave everything behind, we receive our invitation to do the same. Jacob's wrestling match becomes my very own wrestling encounter. Joseph's pit-to-palace journey becomes the hope for every dreamer.

This parallel with ancient Israel prior to David's reign as king is where I believe we are in the Western church today. The past 100 years of American Christianity in particular have made these ancient parallels come alive in my own heart.

Whether it is the stories of perversion or greed of today's compromised priesthood or seeing the erection of political personality monuments of ministry empires like King Saul, we are in desperate need of change. We can even look at the current prophetic movement in America and, like Samuel, watch modern prophets struggle to leave the political crowds of Saul to embrace the Davids who can only be found in obscure places.

I reveal these parallels of the past not primarily to expose the current corrupt religious systems of our day, but more importantly to awaken hope within those of you who find yourself in the reality of these broken systems and relationships. I want to encourage those who are Presence obsessed that this will turn into the greatest moment of seeing God's Presence invade our day.

Don't let fear tell you that the current shaking happening in our nation and religious system has caught Abba off guard and somehow the Kingdom is in a setback. No! This is a perfect scenario for Yahweh's Davids to emerge on the scene.

You and me, we were born for such a time as this!

As we connect the dots of a failed system of religion, may we not lose heart. We must learn from our mistakes, disconnect from these systems of thinking, and awaken to the reality that God's Presence is enough.

So what is the answer for a nation whose religious system helped lead them to its demise?

It's a shepherd boy in the fields of obscurity, learning to faithfully play his harp to the audience of One.

This little boy had no clue that while the religious system in his nation was crumbly, Yahweh was raising him up to be a Presence-obsessed leader who would restore greatness to the nation.

He would not be trained for the priesthood or raised in the school of the prophets, nor would he carry within the legitimate bloodline to be considered a king in Israel. Yet Yahweh found within this shepherd boy the heart of one who hungered for one thing—the Presence of God.

While many seek to see the Kingdom of God invade the West by way of our well-oiled machines of church production led by thought leaders "anointed" in the higher halls of learning, could we admit that it has not had its intended impact upon the culture?

We are living in an hour when the prophetic has been hijacked by American Christians who neatly package and polish the prophetic with Babylonian business principles and the haughtiness of academia.

I do not make this statement to excuse myself or others from scholarly work; however, academia has found a home among Spirit-filled circles only to make our hearts dull. People have become numb to the once heart-piercing words of "thus says the Lord."

While many long to find credibility among the halls of "higher" learning or be accepted among the masses, Yahweh still looks for those who hunger for His Presence to lead the way—leaders who will declare, "This one thing will I seek." Leaders who, even in failure, do not concern themselves with how they look in front of the people. We go to God saying, "Cast me not away from Your Presence and take not Your Holy Spirit from me."

David is the answer for a nation when their religious system has failed them. David is a Presence-obsessed leader who believes that his nation can be great again, not because of the founders' ideas but because he will make Yahweh's Presence a priority once again in his life.

In his pursuit of seeing the Presence of God restored to his life, David's greatest difficulty is that the protocol for hosting the Presence of God has been lost because of poor leadership. David will soon begin the journey but quickly find that he has inherited a protocol from people who did not know the Lord.

Assumptions and Adjustments

David asked the question of how to bring the Presence of God back, but he failed to take the time to question the current paradigm of hosting God's Presence. He did not discover Yahweh's original intent for how the Ark of God was to be carried. The mistake of not pursuing the heart of Yahweh before moving the Ark would soon prove to be deadly.

Many times we fail to discover Yahweh's original intent because we just assume that what we have inherited from previous generations is enough. If it worked for them then it must be for us. However, while we should learn from previous generations, each generation must seek to have their own relationship with God that is not dependent upon the traditions of man alone, but the standard of God that has been passed down through generations.

Being raised up under a political king who cared only about what he looked like in front of the people, David assumed that choice men, large crowds, good music, and a new cart would be appropriate for carrying the Presence back to Jerusalem. This is certainly a mistake we are repeating today.

Because we are a generation raised under the influence of traveling prophets and political kings, we are still convinced that choice men, large crowds, good music, and a new cart are what pleases the Lord.

I want to begin by saying there is nothing wrong with inviting "important" people to church. Everyone needs the gospel and biblical community. There is nothing wrong with large crowds, as I have in my past led a large ministry. Good music is always preferred, and David made sure to hire *skilled* musicians to play around the Ark of His Presence.

However, I think we believe that the Lord will overlook our lack of daily hunger if we do extravagant things for Him occasionally. Israel didn't need a large gathering to restore the Presence of God in their nation. They needed the daily obedience of a faithful priesthood to see His Presence restored.

The beginnings of David's journey are where we are today in Western Christianity. His assumption in his day is our popular conference Christianity today. We, like David, think God is impressed with our idea of choice men. These are not necessarily the people God has chosen; they're just the people we deem important based upon Babylonian metrics of success. Maybe it's because they are incredibly gifted and talented or have a great influence on social media. There's nothing wrong with that, but it's not the answer for who should stand before a generation to lead them into the Presence of God.

Do we dare admit that choice men with gifts and talents are used in our day to garner large crowds because we have agreed to Babylon's metrics in playing the numbers game as this generation's definition of success?

God is not concerned with crowds; He wants faithful priests. If it's true that the compromised priests could pervert a nation, then faithful priests can transform a nation.

David was a man of war and a skilled musician. His initial order was to gather troops and others who were skillful with their instruments. But David soon learned that Yahweh had an order to hosting His Presence that went beyond his preferences. David had to make adjustments.

Up until David's day, because of the hardness of Israel's heart, they saw and used the Ark of the Covenant as a weapon of war, so of course as a man of war there should be a large gathering of troops. And it would be absolutely insulting to David as a skilled musician to not have the best singers and musicians performing around the Ark.

However, Yahweh was not looking for troops for war; He was looking for lovers who knew how to worship. He doesn't want to be reduced to something we use like an instrument of war; He is Someone we host. This might even be hard for some to hear, because we have made singers and musicians the highlight of our gatherings today, but Yahweh was not looking for skilled musicians and singers.

Yahweh is longing for something more, something generational, and something Eden-like.

Today, many feel that we have to stay up with the latest trends, looking to the worship top 40 to determine what the people long to hear. My question then is, "Who is the audience?" Have we forgotten that when we gather we aren't performing for the crowd? We are supposed to lead people into their priestly roles of properly honoring the Presence of the Lord instead of entertaining them so they will show up at our next gathering.

What's trending and loud noise, no matter how skilled, cannot replace our priestly responsibility.

Last and maybe the most dangerous of David's mistakes was that he had a new cart built for the Ark of God's Presence to rest upon. What's the big deal about a cart? After all, that is how David found the Ark of God to begin with.

I don't believe David did this intentionally, but we know from scripture that there was only one purpose for carts, according to the standards God gave Moses, and that was to carry only the common things of the tabernacle. There is nothing common about His Presence, and Yahweh was about to reveal that in a very significant way.

While I do not believe that David did this on purpose, it does speak to us today. What are we doing today as living carriers of His Presence? What have we inherited as our standard from a compromised priesthood, political kings, or, even worse, those who do not know Him?

The new cart is our man-made systems, preferences, and programs in our attempt to build something for the purpose of convenience in a casual Christian culture. We would rather build new buildings, enhance our technology, and bring the comforts of luxury to the people, not realizing our new carts will not cover up the fact that people have forsaken their role as priests unto God.

As John Wesley said, "It is not new metods we need, but new fire." Like the call of Leviticus 6:13, remember—the fire must be kept burning on the altar at all times. It must never go out. It's a daily, intentional pursuit of God that helps us carry His Presence into each day.

We can't just build something absent of His ways and expect God to hitch on to what we are doing. The prophet Jeremiah calls us to look for the old paths, and yet we settle for new carts. However, nothing can replace the necessity of the priesthood.

David's initial pursuit of restoring God's Presence absolutely was influenced by a lack of godly leadership present within Israel. Even worse, he had Israel carry the Presence of God like their enemy did.

Do We Carry His Presence Like the Philistines?

Long before David ever put the Ark on a new cart, the Philistines did.

Earlier in our story, I introduced you to the compromised priesthood of Eli and his two sons, Hophni and Phinehas. One day the sons carried the Ark of God's Presence into battle thinking that a piece of furniture alone would secure them the victory in war.

However, the day Israel went to war against the Philistines in the city of Aphek—the same city where Saul and his son Jonathan would later die as well—the Ark of God was taken from them. This became the initial witness of decades of dysfunctional leadership within Israel. Yahweh taught them a valuable lesson: "I will not accompany anything built by a man unless they follow My order."

Even though the Philistines only had the Ark for a short period of time, it was enough to change how God's Presence would be treated for many years to come.

Who were the Philistines? I'm not talking about where they were from, but what was their mindset? The word *Philistine* in Hebrew means "immigrant," from the root word *Philistia*, which means "land of the sojourners, rolling, or migratory." These were a people driven by ambition who did not care to have roots or to be planted.

The Philistines were driven by materialism and financial gain. They were a culture that despised intellect and artistic culture. They did not take the Ark of God because they cared anything about the Presence of God or beauty; this was a financial asset to them.

Very quickly, they discovered that the Ark of God's Presence was not going to be reduced to monetary gain. God's Presence in their midst caused chaos to enter their world in the form of hemorrhoids. While this story is very strange to say the least, it reveals a powerful truth—you will spend your days straining and striving to carry the weight of His Presence until you learn how to reorder your life.

When the Presence of God is brought into our world, it demands a reordering of the way we do life.

Their answer to the situation was to build a new cart, tie it to some oxen, put a small gift with it, and send it back to Israel. They built this new cart and sent His Presence away so that they could conveniently continue life the way it was before His Presence came.

They didn't want the Presence of God to mess with their financial situation. They didn't want to change the way that they thought. Their decision to build a cart for the Ark was solely out of convenience and to secure their way of life.

Have we done the same? Do we carry the Presence of God like the Philistines? Have we stopped long enough in the name of honoring the Lord to make sure we haven't just accepted models and traditions that were created by men in the church for the convenience of the people, instead of what most honors the glory of God?

What have we been doing in the name of convenience to get people joined to what we have created that is keeping people from making the revolutionary decisions to properly host the Presence of God in their own lives?

Convenience Christianity must come to an end. We can't afford to carry His Presence like the Philistines, because encounters are coming to this generation that are going to redefine what life and the local expression of the church should look like.

His Presence is coming to ruin our ways, trash our schedules, and we are going to inherit the lifestyle of those who have been baptized in the fire of His furious love!

We must heed the warning of Jesus to Peter when He said, "For your heart is not set on God's plans but man's!" He wants to deliver us from the mediocre life of convenience so that we stop making decisions about life on something as inferior as a geographical location, the promise of a job, and the false security of money.

Abba in His goodness is about to let a shaking happen in the life of David's generation to expose any Philistine tendencies within. These tendencies may not have been in their hearts purposefully, but it's all they knew from previous generations before them that never stopped long enough to honor and find out how God wanted to be hosted.

Abba in His goodness is going to let that shaking happen in our day as well. He does not want us to be reduced to immigrants guided by materialism, unwilling to change our thinking, or letting us live in the lie of "convenience."

This Philistine model of convenience is about to be exposed along with the influence of a compromised priesthood and political king. This is why we need moments on the threshing floor of God. A time to find roots, a place to renew our mind, and find abundant life as it should be lived in His Presence.

Nacon's Threshing Floor

David has two men leading the way, Uzzah and Ahio, who were two young men who grew up in Abinadab's home. We will look more into the life of Abinadab in the next section; however, these young men had been around the Ark of God for many years and were expected to understand how to lead the procession back to its rightful place in Jerusalem.

Uzzah's Hebrew name means "strength" and Ahio's name means "brotherly." This points us to the reality of today's Christian culture, where we depend upon the gifts, talents, and strength of men to steer mindless oxen into what man desires instead of prepared priests who know what God wants.

However, this party was about to come to a halt. The Ark of God was moving, music was playing, people were dancing, and all of a sudden the oxen who were leading the new cart carrying the Ark of God stumbled on the threshing floor. A threshing floor is known as a halting place. It is a hard, level spot where the reapers separate the wheat from the chaff. This prophetic spot is where God revealed the difference between His ways and our ways.

It was there at the threshing floor where Uzzah reached out his hand to steady the Ark of God, and when he touched it, he was killed. The worst mistake we can make in this journey is to reach out in our own strength when our carts stumble to steady what Yahweh is clearly shaking. Instead, we must take this moment to prep for the long haul with Abba and ask what He desires.

This journey can't be continued in the convenience of what we have built, nor can we continue to stare at the people in the front to lead us fully into this journey. We all must take responsibility to be prepared to carry His Presence into our cities.

This stumble on the threshing floor is about to uncover many things for David, but the first thing it reveals is that His Presence cannot be handled in a common way.

The threshing floor certainly exposed many things, but even greater is what it was about to reveal. *Nacon* in Hebrew means "enduring preparation." We too find ourselves in a moment of great preparation; let's not miss this same moment in our day. Will we approach His Presence casually, which can result in spiritual death, or will we stop and honor Him enough to ask how He wants to walk with us personally and corporately?

Nacon's threshing floor is our invitation into revival. Will we embrace the invitation and allow what Abba is doing to be such a big deal that it allows Him to come to rearrange our worlds? Will we finally surrender our convenient and common approach to His Presence and once again ask what moves His heart?

A Common
Mistake

The sad reality is that Uzzah was raised in the house of Abinadab. Abinadab was the man who received the Presence of God after the Philistines sent it back to Israel. The Bible says that Abinadab guarded the Presence of God. Unfortunately for Uzzah, what you learn in guarding the Ark as a relic is very different from what you learn hosting the Ark of His Presence.

Uzzah had been around the Ark of God for many years. Yet this was not a moment to guard the Ark; this was a moment to host Him. Just because you have been around the Presence of God for years doesn't mean you know how Yahweh wants to be hosted. He is not a relic to be studied but a Person to be hosted. You cannot reach out in the moment of shaking and try to guard it. This is the sin of familiarity.

May we not make the mistake of Uzzah and, in the moment of shaking, reach out in a common way to protect our way of doing things. If it's shaking, let it shake. How many times do we go through a moment of shaking, and instead of letting God reveal to us the problem, we go and try to fix it in our own strength?

At Nacon's threshing floor, the system of convenience was exposed and Uzzah's common approach to God's Presence was judged. Now David knows he must send everyone home.

This is where I believe we are prophetically in the West. A.W. Tozer said, "The first step down for any church is taken when it surrenders its high opinion of God."[3] God will never allow us to experience His glory with a common approach! Hebrews 12:26-29 says:

> But now he [Yahweh] has promised, "Once and for all I will not only shake the systems of the world, but also the unseen powers in the heavenly realm!" Now this phrase "once and for all" clearly indicates the final removal of things that are shaking, that is, the old order, so only what is unshakable will remain. Since we are receiving our rights to an unshakable kingdom we should be extremely thankful and offer God the purest worship that delights his heart as we lay down our lives in absolute surrender, filled with awe. For our God is a holy, devouring fire!

In 2020, we entered into a moment of shaking. Our way of doing things has been exposed, and God has used the shaking of our man-made systems to send us home to rethink how we should be doing things. It's time to make enduring decisions and long-term commitments for how we plan to rearrange our worlds to properly restore God's Presence back to our homes, cities, and nations.

For too long we have taken our cues from those who guarded His Presence as a relic instead of taking our cues from those who have hosted His Presence through an intimate relationship. Something needs to shift.

It's a tragedy to ask for God's Presence to come into our lives only to treat Him casually. What halted the journey was the failure to seek God and a common approach to His Presence!

God's glory will always remain hidden from the casual approach to His Presence. What mysteries are yet to be revealed, what glory is in a holding pattern because we seek God on our terms? We need to say yes to a life of honor and intentionality toward God's Presence.

Apostle Aaron Smith, from Gates of Zion in Mobile, Alabama, said, "The glory is the goal. You can only get to the glory by honor. You cannot have real honor without love. You can only stay in this place of love, honor, and glory by peace."

Did you catch it? You can only get to the glory by way of honor.

What is the glory? It is the transformative dimension of God in the earth where God's preeminence is made known among men.

That's the realm we want to live in. But there can be no common approach.

We need this time of shaking to once again recapture the proper honor for God's Presence.

Honor is valuing, precious, and weighty. Dishonor means to treat as common or ordinary, to not esteem.

God will protect the mystery of His glory from the common gaze of dishonor, but those who can honor God's Presence with uncommon devotion will be the ones who keep the gate of glory open to their generation.

What are we holding back from our day because of a common gaze?

Although Uzzah died at the threshing floor for his common approach, the shaking at Nacon's threshing floor was not just judgment—it was His mercy to expose the system of religion that had been created to keep Abba and man from their seamless union.

Abba never intended for things like buildings, instruments, and conferences to carry Him. He desires to dwell and rest in and upon His people.

While writing this book, we are two years into a global pandemic. This is not something I believe originated in the heart of God, but it did not catch Him by surprise. However, I believe the Lord actually took what satan meant for evil and used it for good to place us in a moment when we should consider our ways.

While many looked at the earlier orders of lockdowns as captivity, I had a strong sense from the Lord that these times of shutdown, quarantine, and social distancing were placing us in the incubator of a new world.

His Presence is in the midst of this shakeup, calling us into a new wineskin, new blueprints, a new order, a new way of doing life, and back to His original intent.

The carts we have built in organized religion have been exposed. The institutions and denominations we created were our attempts to make the Kingdom convenient and safe. Abba is asking us to rearrange our world in a way that reflects His—life centered around His Presence.

We can't go back to normal. Sunday/Wednesday church and conference Christianity can't be the answer. Just look through the past decades of this style of Christian life and tell me—has the culture been changed? *No!*

We can't leave this time of shaking and give the West a version of the church little better than we had before the pandemic began. The earth is groaning for the manifestation of the sons of God.

We must realize we are at Nacon's threshing floor being asked a very important question. Will we continue to sacrifice our sons to keep our systems or will we allow Holy Spirit to expose our systems in order that our sons can restore Presence back to our cities?

A Prophetic Witness for a New Day

In fear of the Lord's anger, David halted the journey, sent everyone home, and ordered the Ark of God to be placed within the home of Obed-Edom. It remained there for three months and the Bible says, "and the Lord blessed Obed-Edom and his entire household" (2 Sam. 6:11 NLT).

It was during this time that David went home and discovered the original intent for how man was to properly host the Ark of God. But while David was learning the protocol, a small family would become a prophetic indicator to a nation of what God was about to do.

So what do you do when leaders are unsure exactly how to prepare for the new day? Don't focus on what a sincere leader has not yet learned; you must learn to host His Presence in your home. That prophetic witness will become the confirmation to sincere leaders in the days to come.

What happened during those 90 days at Obed-Edom's house?

Obed-Edom was a small prophetic window into what the Lord would soon reveal. God was not interested in crowds. He wanted families in devotion.

Obed in Hebrew means "the servant who honors God in a right way." Obed-Edom was a Levite. Jewish rabbinical literature says that Obed-Edom would light a candle twice a day, once in the morning and once in the evening, to honor the Ark of God's Presence.

Because of Obed-Edom's honor toward the Lord, his wife and all eight daughters-in-law bore children during those three months. The Lord was showing honor toward those who had released honor to Him and took one family's devotion to reverse the curse of the compromised priesthood.

Obed-Edom's simple life of devotion in his home became the prophetic witness to David during his time of discovery—God was pleased and it was time to proceed in his journey to restore the Presence of God to the city of Jerusalem.

Yes, David needed to learn proper protocol for handling the Ark of God, but more importantly, Yahweh was making a statement to all of Israel that big crowds, loud music, and important people are not what Yahweh desires. He longs for men to honor His Presence in their homes with their families.

Maybe you are reading this and failed to understand the moment we were given during the recent pandemic. Many church gatherings were sporadic; our old way of doing things was disrupted. But the good news is, you can still create a new normal in your home.

You can become this generation's Obed-Edom while a nation desperately needs to be awakened to the reality of His Presence.

You can start by honoring the Lord morning and evening with your family. Acknowledge His Presence when you grab your coffee and Bible in the morning or while you are sitting with family around the dinner table at night.

What seems like simple devotion within the walls of your home is going to begin to shine a beacon of light to church leaders who are searching for a new path to seeing our nation return to God.

I have grown up in this conference Christianity we have experienced for decades now in our nation. We have filled churches, arenas, and stadiums only to see our nation continue to decline. We, like David, thought that if we gathered crowds surely God would be pleased and turn our nation around.

It was not until David sent the crowd home and put the Ark back in a house where a family would honor His Presence well that the tide began to turn. We are in the same circumstances today. Conference Christianity does not work!

I spent years hosting major Christian conferences, inviting in the best speakers and worship leaders in the country. Four to five thousand people would gather, and weeks later I would go speak at churches who would attend our conferences only to realize they needed another encounter.

What good is it for us to host large gatherings and create an atmosphere for people if they are not willing to go back to their homes and home church and cultivate an atmosphere of honor for the Presence of God?

Conference and event-driven Christianity produces an unhealthy codependency upon larger ministries to do for them what they should be doing for themselves. Or worse, we put it into the minds of smaller churches that if they don't have the lights, technology, or ability to invite in celebrity Christians then they will have no chance of experiencing the move of God.

God is speaking to our generation through Obed-Edom today: "I don't need lights, fog, technology, or your favorite worship leader—bring a candle beside your chair with a Bible, notepad, and a heart ready to encounter Me and I will come!"

This was my experience after leaving popular Christianity in 2015. I moved our family to the middle of nowhere South Carolina, to a small home, and joined ourselves to a small church in the woods that was hungry for the Presence of God.

We had no smoke or lights, conference speakers, or famous worship leaders. But we had a hunger to host the Presence of God well. The corporate expression was being fed by houses filled with families who made their lives evolve around one thing. God was invading our homes, bedrooms, cars, and dinners.

It was there I began to learn that God was not looking for crowds; He was looking for homes where the family altar is restored. Where fathers' hearts are turned to their children instead of their careers. Families were being restored not because of counseling, but encounters.

This is why we needed a Nacon's threshing floor moment in our generation. We need to make long-path decisions, enduring decisions to come out of the failing models of systemic religion and bring Jesus back to the center of our lives, homes, and churches.

We can't afford to go back to normal and embrace any system of religious convenience. A new order has come, a new wineskin ready to receive the new wine reserved for this day! God forbid we just go back to Sunday-only Christianity in the American church. We need to make Jesus the focal point, and when we do, He will show us how to establish His Presence back in our cities and nations.

David Receives Adjustments from the Lord

For because you did not do it the first time, the Lord our God broke out against us, because we did not consult Him about the proper order (1 Chronicles 15:13 NKJV).

David went back to Jerusalem to seek the Lord following the death of Uzzah. Yes, Uzzah died because of his common approach, but more importantly, David knew that he was responsible for Uzzah's ignorance of properly handling the Ark of God. David failed to seek the Lord for the proper order of how God's Presence should be hosted.

David's negligence in seeking the Lord not only cost the city three more months of the absence of the Presence of God, but it also cost him the life of one he was responsible to lead.

If you are a church leader reading this, we should sense the fear of the Lord in this verse. Have we truly sought the Lord for His order and direction for what He wants to do? Have we truly sought the Lord so that the people we are called to lead are ready to become carriers of His Presence? Or have some become spiritually dead because of our negligence to seek the face of God and bring to them the prophetic direction of the Lord?

Will we continue to follow in the footsteps of insecure political leaders like Saul, who cared so much about his appearance before the people that he never once considered recapturing the Ark of God during his entire reign as king?

David had many assumptions when he started this journey, but because of the halting at Nacon's threshing floor, David knew it was time to seek the Lord to make adjustments. He named the place where Uzzah was killed "Perez Uzzah" or "Breach of Uzzah" because an act of failing to observe the ways of God caused the journey to be stopped.

But the Lord has called us in Isaiah 58 to be "repairers of the breach," which is a call to raise up the foundations of many generations. I believe we are in an hour when the Lord is going to give us keys to go back and repair the mistakes of previous generations that have kept His Presence from invading cities.

We find David's discoveries in 1 Chronicles 15. No one but the Levites can carry the ark of the Lord, because the Lord has chosen them. And not just any Levites, but they had to be from the house of Kohath.

How did David discover this? He would not know the proper order without diving back into his Presence obsession. I can see David inquiring of the Lord in prayer and with the help of others diving back into the scriptures. How I wish we would do the same today. We have so neglected an intimate relationship with Jesus through the Holy Spirit that most have forsaken the word of God in this generation. We don't even realize when we misrepresent Him to those who look at our lives.

While I am a man who believes there is nothing more powerful than a divine encounter with Jesus, I will never shy away from the fact that those who had powerful encounters also had a strong relationship with Yahweh through His word and were faithful in the place of prayer.

A simple reading of scripture unlocked the divine protocol for David to confidently regroup and finish the journey of bringing the Presence of God back to Jerusalem. I'm sure David was surprised once the blueprint was uncovered. It had nothing to do with music, the military, or choice men. The Lord was looking for a family under the order of a certain father to carry the Presence of God back to Jerusalem.

Levites from the House of Kohath

Then he commanded, "No one except the Levites may carry the Ark of God. The Lord has chosen them to carry the Ark of the Lord and to serve him forever" (1 Chronicles 15:2 NLT).

David's first discovery during his time of seeking the Lord following the halting at Nacon's threshing floor is that the Lord desires men, not carts, to carry Him. His Presence was always to rest on men, not on our systems.

So who are these men whom God asked to carry His Presence?

The Levites descended from Jacob and Leah's third son. The Levites were divided into three clans: Gershonites, Kohathites, and Merarites. Each clan had specific duties involving the care of the tabernacle and temple.

The setting apart of the tribe as a whole is recorded after the incident with the golden calf (see Exod. 32). When Moses called for the faithful, the Levites rallied around him (see Exod. 32:26-29). They demonstrated their faithfulness by slaying the apostate from among the nation.

As a part of their ordination, the Levites represented the first-born of the nation owed to God for the Passover deliverance (see Num. 3:40-51; Exod. 13:1-2). The tribe existed as living sacrifices, from which their role as religious functionaries arose.[4]

These men were prepared priests who would not forsake the Lord. But the thing that sticks out the most to me is that they took responsibility to host God's Presence even when God was not "moving."

When Israel traveled through the wilderness, they followed God's Presence in the cloud by day and the pillar of fire by night. All of Israel would follow the manifestation of God when He was moving, but the Levites did more than just follow—they learned to host Him well.

Anyone can follow God in the move of God, but what do you do when it seems like nothing is happening? The Levites did not go back to life as usual; they began setting up the tent of meeting, filling the lampstand with oil, cooking the showbread, and offering sacrifices to the One who had called them.

If we are the generation who is going to restore God's Presence back to our cities, then we have to be those who don't just follow Him when we see the manifestations of His Presence. We must set our hearts to host Him well when we don't have any evidence that He is moving.

I see a generation that can enter into the Presence of God no matter what is happening or not happening in a church or on a platform. I see a generation that doesn't need cheerleaders in the front of the church because they have prepared themselves in secret. They have found Him to be close when no one else believes He is near.

Yahweh is calling for a generation of prepared priests, but the protocol gets more specific—He has chosen Levites from the house of Kohath. *Kohath* in Hebrew means "those who ally themselves to the assembly."

David's discovery of the proper order unlocks a powerful picture for us today. No one is called to carry His Presence alone. Yes, we need Levites, but we need Levites from a particular house and from a particular father.

We are standing in the small beginnings of this Presence movement sweeping the globe. However, those who are going to be carriers of His Presence will not be mavericks disconnected from the local church expression who set out to do great exploits of their own. Those are the "Jesus and me got our own thing going on" people. No, the protocol is you must be closely joined to fathers and family.

This Presence movement is going to be individuals who know they are loved by Abba, who have said yes to the lifestyle of devotion, and who are just as equally committed to being joined to the family of God and submitted to spiritual fathers. God's Presence was never intended to be carried alone. I believe that is why God ordained a particular family to carry it.

It was those who were allied to the assembly who got to carry His Presence personally. Yes, each individual gets to experience God in their own way, but not without being vitally joined to the family. We see this picture plainly in Acts 2:1-3:

On the day Pentecost was being fulfilled, all the disci-
ples were gathered in one place. Suddenly they heard
the sound of a violent blast of wind rushing into the
house from out of the heavenly realm. The roar of the
wind was so overpowering it was all anyone could bear!
Then all at once a pillar of fire appeared before their
eyes. It separated into tongues of fire that engulfed
each one of them.

The birth of the church began with those who were committed to gathering together, and those who gathered were all personally filled with the Holy Spirit. In a moment, not only did the Holy Spirit fill them with the very life of God, but they were instantaneously turned into family. We must be committed to assemble with the family of God.

We are moving away from the institutional model where we become members of a brand and building, and we are coming back to the relational model of the book of Acts where we become members of His body.

For his "body" has been formed in his image and is
closely joined together and constantly connected as
one. And every member has been given divine gifts
to contribute to the growth of all; and as these gifts
operate effectively throughout the whole body, we
are built up and made perfect in love (Ephesians
4:16).

We are being called to be closely connected, contributing to the growth of all, so we can all be built up together into the image of Christ, which is the Presence of God.

In an hour when we see governments consider large corporations and liquor stores essential to people during a pandemic while churches are considered problematic, we cannot back down from assembling together. It is the church united that releases the image of God into the culture around us.

> *This is not the time to pull away and neglect meeting together, as some have formed the habit of doing. In fact, we should come together even more frequently, eager to encourage and urge each other onward* (Hebrews 10:25).

Those who carry His Presence in this hour will be those who have learned how to be joined to the assembly of the family of God. While I am calling you to leave behind old, dead religious systems, I am not calling you into the isolation of deconstruction. We are being called into an authentic version of family that was modeled for us in the scriptures' account of the early church.

The call of those who will carry His Presence is a call to "Be devoted to tenderly loving your fellow believers as members of one family. Try to outdo yourselves in respect and honor of one another" (Rom. 12:10). We are called to "Take advantage of every opportunity to be a blessing to others, especially to our brothers and sisters in the family of faith!" (Gal. 6:10).

For those who have wandered away from the family, the apostle James calls us as members of God's beloved family, "We must go after the one who wanders from the truth and bring him back" (James 5:19). That's a part of my assignment in this book. To come after those of you who have forsaken the assembling of family because you were hurt by the institutionalized Christianity of the West.

You were right to leave the system of religion, but don't get stuck in isolation. If you want the fruit of the New Testament, you cannot do that alone. You must be joined to the family of God.

We need another upper-room people in this hour who are committed to Jesus, submitted to leaders, preferring one another, operating in the order of fathers and sons, and always endeavoring to keep the unity of the Spirit in the bond of peace.

God is saying to us in this hour that for too long we have looked to choice men, crowds, and skilled musicians to bring the Ark of His Presence back to our cities, and it has caused many Uzzahs to fall by a common approach.

What King David began to discover in the days following the death of Uzzah is a discovery we desperately need today. God is looking for families, which we will talk about more later in the book, who will say yes to hosting the Presence of Jesus extravagantly if we intend to see His Presence restored to our cities.

More Than He Asked For

Once David discovered the protocol for carrying the Ark of God, he knew that if a common approach halted the journey, it would take an uncommon pursuit to start again. Many times we read stories and miss very significant pieces to the process. But David did not just stop at doing just enough. Now that protocol was restored, David could offer more than what was asked for by way of honor.

> *And so it was, when those bearing the ark of the Lord had gone six paces, that he sacrificed oxen and fatted sheep* (2 Samuel 6:13 NKJV).

There is no biblical requirement for sacrificing oxen and lambs every six steps in order to move the Ark of God. But David commissioned the oxen to be sacrificed as a sign that he was never going to allow someone or something else to take the responsibility to shoulder His Presence away from the priesthood.

Oxen may have started the journey before, but now that protocol was inherited, David felt they must put on the altar anything that was keeping them from bearing the weight of His Presence themselves.

If we are going to see the Presence of God invade this generation, we must make sure we don't depend upon someone or something to do for us what we should take responsibility to do ourselves. This is the essence of the life of devotion—to have an intentional approach to come under the weight of all the Father has for us.

For too long we have lived codependent upon the anointing of others and the corporate gathering, and we have failed to cultivate the oil of intimacy in the secret place with Jesus.

Give Him more than He asked for.

It may be more than what was asked for, but David's motivation was honor! You can never go wrong with honor when it was the common, careless approach of dishonor that impeded their journey before.

This approach is always met with, "It doesn't take all that," from those bound in religion. These people are the ones satisfied with doing just enough to be church attendees. To check the box of Sunday-only Christianity. But we were not born to be led by those bound by the confines of Sunday-only religion.

If you are going to say yes to being a carrier of His Presence, you will have to disconnect from the advice of well-intentioned people who are satisfied by the status-quo American Christianity that entertains people with good music and self-help sermons.

While I am extremely thankful for the well-intentioned people who brought me this far on the journey, I can no longer rely upon people who say we need only go so far. May we take our shoes off like Moses and stand with nothing between us and holy ground.

It was Moses who had an encounter with the uncommon Presence of God in a bush that was burning but was not consumed. As Moses stared into this miraculous sight, the voice of God gave him a simple request that most would think was insignificant: "Take your shoes off."

The Western church's response to such a request in our post-modern society is, "God, it's just a pair of shoes," or my favorite, "But everyone has shoes." But to the one who is hungry for His Presence, you are willing to lay down things that most people consider normal.

We respond with the writer of Hebrews 12:1, to lay aside every weight and sin, because a person hungry for God's Presence is not concerned with sin. On the other side of Calvary we lose our sin-consciousness and we want to make sure there is nothing weighing us down from ascending into the Presence of God as we are intended to.

My spiritual father, Damon Thompson, says, "There must be a higher commitment to a new standard of devotion in order for us to inherit a higher awareness of His Presence." Will you say yes to that elevated commitment to do more than He even asks for or what others say is too much?

Yahweh is looking for a people with an uncommon devotion to introduce the world to His uncommon Presence.

The Table of Tension

Here is where I feel we are prophetically as a people who are hungry for the Presence of God. It will take our extravagance to expose those straddling the fence about whether or not we need a new wineskin.

In Luke 7, Jesus accepted an invitation to come into the house of religion so that one broken box could reveal the true intentions of the host. It's time for you and I to recognize whether or not we are in right place. You will know it by what the host does when the broken box of worship is lavished on the feet of Jesus.

The Presence movement is beginning to cover the earth, and when His Presence shows up, it creates tension among groups and institutions, and it challenges our preferences. Just take a glance throughout the four gospels—anytime Jesus shows up it causes tension. Could you imagine the tension when Jesus halted a funeral procession in Nain and told a mother not to weep for her son?

Can you imagine the tension Jesus created in the hearts of the religious after they dropped their stones and had to walk away from an adulterous woman whom Moses' law said should be stoned?

What about when Jesus dismissed the professional wailers weeping in Jairus' house so that He could bring his daughter back to life? Could you imagine the tension in those who got dismissed from the room?

I know we try to shy away from things that create tension or confrontation. It seems like no one wants to rock the boat or go against the grain, but the Presence of Jesus is coming into situations all over this nation and it's going to cause tension.

Tension because we have settled for being spectators of anointed ministry. Tension because He wants to do something brand new, yet we want to preserve the old. Tension because the hungry want to be equipped instead of entertained. Tension because He doesn't want you to live vicariously through your pastor's relationship with God; He wants you to walk with Him yourself.

That's why I believe the Lord is setting up a table of tension in the house of religion.

Take a trip with me into the courtyard of Simon the Pharisee. It was a beautiful day in Israel, the sun shining and the table set. The fountains were full, and a lovely garden of flowers was on full display. Men and women were moving hastily across the courtyard to prepare for a special occasion. Each seat was arranged—the host, esteemed guests, and of course a place for the honored guest. It was what we would call today a red-carpet event. Some of the most prominent leaders of their day would be present to host a young Galilean phenomenon.

The host of this auspicious gathering was Simon the Pharisee. Despite the bitter tension between the Pharisees and this ragtag bunch from Galilee, Simon somehow managed to bring Jesus to his table. The differences between these two groups were no secret. Jesus called these men hypocrites, evil, adulterous, serpents, a generation of vipers, fools, blind guides, and white-washed tombs full of dead men's bones.

Jesus said, "Beware of the leaven of the Pharisees" because you can listen to their teaching but shouldn't follow their example—everything they do is for a show. Jesus continued scolding their pride when He told the people how much they love sitting at the heads of tables in banquets and the seats of honor inside the synagogue. With so much tension, we must ask two questions—why would Simon invite Jesus to his house and why would Jesus accept the invitation?

Was Simon interested in knowing Jesus personally? Or maybe he was hired as a private investigator to help bring more charges against this rebellious Man claiming to be the Christ? Considering Jesus' description of these men, I have concluded along with other historians that Simon was a collector of celebrities. Inviting this young Galilean sensation was nothing more than an attempt to patronize Jesus to garner a crowd!

In the church today we have followed Simon the Pharisee's pattern for church growth. We create beautiful courtyards, offering the best religious entertainment men and women can find. We collect celebrities, not caring whether we know them intimately or not. No one questions the fruit of their lives. If their gift is drawing crowds and moving rooms, we will create the most beautiful courtyard scene we can to host such an event. Is this not happening in the American church today? Set up the table, put out the best linens and utensils, invite the most distinguished guests, and let's gather a crowd around our table.

I can see Simon's intention—he isn't interested in his guest; he likes to host the crowd, to be the center of attention. The honored guest is not invited to be recognized but rather to put the host on display. Jesus, knowing these things, was not without discernment. So then why would Jesus, who felt so strongly about the Pharisees, accept the invitation? Was His Presence in a house of religion accepted to create a table of tension?

Was it Christ's mercy that made Him come to Simon's house? Absolutely! But many leaders in the church today make the mistake of Simon, seeing the Presence of Jesus as a validation of the host. We must ask ourselves, what if His Presence comes to expose our invitation? What if He begins to reveal the infrastructure of the house? His acceptance of this request was an invitation in itself.

As a young man, I know enough about His Presence to know that when He comes, it reveals people, their honor, motives, attitudes, and agendas. Secrets manifest, lies are exposed, wolves throw off sheep's clothes, and snakes strike in the heat of His Presence. We cannot see His Presence as only validation of the host. It is an invitation, a provocation to respond rightly to the Presence of God Himself.

The table is set. On one side the Pharisees, with their host sitting at the head of the table across from twelve low-class citizens and Jesus in the seat as the guest of "honor." Psalm 23 speaks of a table that I now call the table of tension: "You prepare a table before me in the presence of my enemies" (Ps. 23:5 NKJV). Here in the courtyard of Simon, with people gathered around, the enemy and the answer for the world are sitting at the same table.

An Unexpected Guest

The meal is laid out with beautiful flowers as accents. The noise of small talk fills the ears of everyone around the table. The gate swings open and in walks an unexpected guest—a prostitute. The religious radar goes off the charts because sin has been detected. But the fact that sin captured their attention in such a high degree of His Presence is an indicator that they lacked appropriate revelation.

Apostle Damon Thompson says, "Religion can find fault in the giver and even measure the value of the gift, but religion cannot see the value of the Recipient."

Religion wanted to expose her reputation. They even questioned Jesus as a prophet because He "could not" receive such adoration from a sinner. But Jesus used this unexpected guest's extravagant devotion to expose their hearts. Jesus leaned over to Simon and said, "I have something to say to you. When I entered your home, you didn't offer Me water to wash the dust from my feet, but she has washed them with her tears and wiped them with her hair. I tell you, her sins, and they are many, have been forgiven, so she has shown Me much love. But a person who is forgiven little shows little love."

I used to think the key to this story was her alabaster box. A special spikenard, a spice from North India near the Himalayas, carried over a thousand miles to be brought to the Middle East. It is believed that this fragrant oil was worth a year's wages. But that was not the key at all. The key was her revelation of the Recipient, and the gift was only a secondary consequence of that revelation. This gift becomes the illustration to us of what a proper response to the revelation of His Presence should be.

An appropriate response is birthed from a proper revelation. The Bible says she knew that Jesus was in the house. That word *knew* can be translated from the Greek as "to perceive, to understand, to know thoroughly, or to know accurately." She wasn't thinking "good teacher"—she was thinking Chain Breaker, Messiah, Deliverer, and Savior! It was her revelation of Jesus that unlocked her extravagance.

Jesus asked His disciples one day, "Who do men say that I am?" If you are familiar with this story, you know this was Peter's moment of brilliance—his admission of Jesus being the Christ, the Son of the living God. Then Jesus said to Peter, "Upon this rock, I will build My church." In other words, "upon this revelation of knowing who I am, I will build My church." He will build His church anywhere there is a present revelation of who He is, whether it's in the house of Simon the Pharisee or the stronghold of a pagan nation. The only requirement is a revelation of who He is!

A Culture of Extravagance

All over the earth, I believe the Lord is coming to houses (churches) like Simon's that are waiting for an uninvited guest to barge in and break their box of extravagant devotion to Jesus. It awakens the heart, exposes the religious, but provides permission for those who have yet to pour out their devotion in such extravagant ways! But I must warn you—if you are going to establish a culture of extravagant worship, you will have to do it in the face of religion.

Can you see it? When this woman came through the gate of the courtyard, historically, the design of the table would have the host as the centerpiece of festivities. So her first look would have come from the religious scorn of Simon the Pharisee. Without hesitation, she ripped the necklace from her neck that held her alabaster box to her chest. Jesus would have been sitting in a relaxed position with His legs tucked underneath Him. Without even seeing His face, she would have to stare into the eyes of Simon while she broke her box on the feet of Jesus.

But when you have an actual revelation, you never yield to the looks of religion. She knew what house she walked into, but more importantly, she knew Who was in the room. Extravagance is the result of your revelation possessing your spirit! I'm sure she heard many stories of what Jesus was capable of doing, from calming seas to raising the dead. But whatever it was that drew her to that moment, she had been overcome by the fact that if she broke her box, He would forgive her sin! What else could she do? It was the only proper response.

The days are upon us when you will not be able to fool other believers in a culture of such extravagance. Excess and extravagance concerning the Presence of Jesus can exist anywhere this is an appropriate revelation. You can't blame your city, your church, or your pastor—these excuses will not work. People who know Him as Jehovah Jireh don't bat an eye at extravagant giving. If you know that He hears our petitions, then extravagant prayer is not unusual. I think you get the point—extravagance proceeds appropriate revelation! If you really know who He is, you know the broken alabaster box is the only proper response!

Simon Learns a Lesson

I'm sure in the midst of such an awkward interruption Simon tried to pull the attention back to his agenda. But it was too late, the fragrance was too strong, and the oil was still fresh on the feet of Jesus and her hair. As silence gripped their hearts, Jesus took the opportunity to teach Simon one more valuable lesson. What she did was not a result of her sin but in response to the revelation of forgiveness.

"She has been forgiven of all her many sins. This is why she has shown Me such extravagant love. But those who assume they have very little to be forgiven for, will love Me very little." Jesus was letting this group of self-righteous leaders know the source of their dishonor was not only their lack of revelation concerning who He was, but they assumed their religion was no worse sin than a prostitute's.

Jesus took the time to let them know their assumption was wrong. There at the table, Jesus put everyone on a level playing field. So many make this same mistake today. People will hear the story of a drug addict, someone molested, or another believer's testimony of rejection, neglect, and abuse, and they'll think that their story is why they are so extravagant. But those of us who have grown up in the church and were good people, feel like Jesus had to pay a different price for them than us.

This is a grand deception that religion places upon those who feel they have no story. This gives many the excuse that if we had a better story, we would be more extravagant. Jesus paid the same price for the good religious church kid as He did for the prostitute. He did not let Simon off the hook, and He will not let us. We do not need a better story; we just need a better revelation of Him!

So What Will We Do with Jesus?

Today we have built incredible edifices—in light of Simon's story, beautiful courtyards. Our leaders, much like Simon, care little about the Presence of Jesus but instead collect celebrities to garner crowds. We search for who is hot, who has the most YouTube views or followers on Instagram to determine our speaker lineup. Like leaves on a fruitless fig, we cover our fruitlessness with lights and haze as clocks lead our worship experience with click tracks. Our current conference-driven franchise models we call "churches" have become red-carpet events for the famous, gifted, and talented.

We no longer ask Abba what He wants; instead, we ask Babylon what works. We have turned to numerical success, with church metrics guiding our decisions, and we look at numbers to find validity. Leaders have conditioned men and women to be enamored with their mission, and we have taught them to rally around the pulpit. Our systemic religion has pushed out seekers of His Presence, and we wonder why we see so much casualness in our current version of Christianity.

If we are not careful, those who will pay the highest price in these days of the move of the Spirit will be those who have been anointed to lead it. We have gathered around anointed ministry for so many years that we have become codependent on it. We live vicariously through their stories and experiences, and when they are done, so are we. With that mentality, we train believers to gather around preachers, and we put pressure on leaders to be our answer. That's when anointed vessels need to correct course and decrease so His Presence can increase. We need not look further than King Uzziah or the anointed cherub lucifer to discover their outcome.

There is a table of tension in the house of religion—the religious spirit face to face with Jesus and extravagant worship. The tension is found in the decision of what side of the table you will be found on. Will it be among the smirks of popular religion, collecting celebrities, gathering around preachers, and enjoying the entertainment of religion? Or will they see you among those who are dripping with the oil of devotion? My prayer is that you will be those who will pour it all out at His feet right in the face of religion.

I hope the pages of this book will bring you to such obsession with His Presence that you will never settle for the inferior idea we have called church. It has cost us more than many are willing to admit; just ask the children of those who gave their lives to building such ministry empires. We must look to scripture and church history for those who have risked it all for their obsession to host Presence properly. We can learn from their mistakes and glean from their breakthroughs.

But my greatest desire is that you will become the lovesick Bride that the next generation will write about. And what will they say to those who answer this call? I hope there is only one word they can use to describe our relationship with Jesus: *obsessed!*

Now looking back at Uzzah, isn't it amazing that a man who had been around the Presence of God his entire life would not know how to properly host the Presence of God, but the hunger for Jesus in the prostitute became a New Testament standard for the proper response to His Presence?

Uzzah died for steadying the Ark, and one prostitute who made a decision to break her alabaster box on the feet of Jesus in extravagant worship set the standard for worship.

It reveals one amazing truth: extravagance is the only proper response to the Presence of Jesus.

The church is never going to properly restore Presence to our cities without those willing to break their boxes on the feet of Jesus in the face of religion. What is the worst that could happen? Someone might ask you to leave their church because of passion for Jesus. It may be the only way for you to realize what kind of government you are under in the church, and it will certainly be the quickest way to find your tribe of people ready to break their box with you.

However, extravagance can only be an expression built on a solid foundation, and in this next section I want to focus on the Levites from the house of Kohath. I believe that God is looking for a family committed to the lifestyle of devotion under the government of fathers. It is the order of fathers and sons, established and enfolded into the family of God, that is the enduring wineskin of the Kingdom of God.

Are you ready for a new blueprint?

A New Blueprint

We are standing in the early days of a global reformation that will be spearheaded by Davids who know they are loved and chosen by God to bring His Presence back to the center of our lives. If you haven't recognized it, I believe 2020 and all the struggles it brought was our time of shaking. That time as difficult as it was, provided a door of grace for us to discover a new blueprint, a new order, a new wineskin.

The power of institutionalism and tradition is being broken and we are recapturing the relational blueprint of the early church. Only the David's, the beloved one can inherit the relational wineskin of the Kingdom who is qualified to carry the weight of His Presence into our cities today.

We recognize the mistakes of a compromised priesthood, the traveling prophets, and political kings. However, real change does not come by placing blame on others or constantly pointing at the mistakes of the past. We must enter into the secret place and inherit a new blueprint for this day.

By now, I hope you sense the desperate need for transition. I'm not just talking to mainstream evangelicals. I'm talking to the awakening and revival camps that are leading the charge in the prayer and prophetic movements.

I'm talking to the prayer movement that has been focused for years on repentance and reconciliation for past mistakes. While I am incredibly thankful that we are learning from history and determined not to repeat our mistakes, we cannot afford to remain focused on living in the past.

I'm talking to the prophetic movement that is always announcing what is coming and, quite honestly, very rarely do we ever inherit what is being announced because we have already jumped into the future for another word. It's one thing to announce it, but someone has to be present enough to receive it and more importantly, manifest it.

While I am incredibly grateful for both the prayer and prophetic movement for reconciling the past and announcing the future, someone has to awaken to what is happening in the present. We have become proficient in stewarding the past and future, but it seems we struggle with being present, and that becomes an extraordinary problem if we are to see a Presence movement sweep the globe.

Again, I honor the pioneers of the modern-day prayer and prophetic movements; however, we are living in a day when someone has to build on what the pioneers paved the way for. But it will take someone present in His Presence to see that happen.

The book of Revelation does not reveal Jesus as just the one who was and who is to come but "who was, and is, and is to come." If we dare to see Jesus become the featured attraction of the nations, we must learn to be present in His Presence! He is doing a new thing, but are we present enough to allow this Presence movement to come forth?

In David's pursuit of restoring God's Presence to his city, he found a blueprint that I believe speaks to our day, especially if you and I believe that God is currently rebuilding the tabernacle of David in this generation. The apostles believed this in their day when James quoted the ancient prophecy of Amos, saying:

> "After these things I will return to you and raise up the tabernacle of David that has fallen into ruin. I will restore and rebuild what David experienced so that all of humanity will be able to encounter the Lord including the gentiles whom I have called to be my very own," says the Lord (Acts 15:16-17).

So if God is raising up the tabernacle of David, then we better pay attention to his journey for restoring Presence to his city because it carries very significant blueprints for us today.

Remember, David realized that our modern-day conference Christianity model was not what pleased God. God was looking for prepared priests from a particular house with a particular father. In David's day, it would have been Levites from the house of Kohath. In our day, I believe it is a kingdom of priests joined to a local kingdom family that is being led by spiritual fathers.

I want to spend some time talking about fathers and family because most of the time, when we think about God raising up a Presence movement, we think in terms of music. If we think the rebuilding of the tabernacle of David is simply about music, we have settled for a very inferior idea of what God's Presence is longing to establish on the earth.

David's journey reveals to us that God intends to be carried by families, not music. Music can certainly be a part, but as we have seen already, had Uzzah been fathered in how to properly host God's Presence his story could have ended much differently.

It might seem strange to you that I would write about fathers and family while speaking to you about restoring God's Presence to cities. However, it will take the order of fathers and sons to birth a true Presence movement if we expect the sons of God to be revealed and the earth to be transformed.

Remember, in the New Covenant we are not talking about tents, buildings, and how to conduct services. When we think "tabernacle of David" today, we should be thinking more about men than music. Because today, we are the dwelling place of God.

We are the tabernacle, the address of God, and the new wineskin. So what I am talking about has to go beyond a reformation of church structure, orders of service, and how long we can flow in music. The reformation of our hearts joined together in Christ becomes His tabernacle.

> *You are rising like the perfectly fitted stones of the temple; and your lives have been built up together upon the foundation laid by the apostles and prophets, and best of all, you are connected to the Head Cornerstone of the building, the Anointed One, Jesus Christ himself! This entire building is under construction and is continually growing under his supervision until it rises up completed as the holy temple of the Lord himself. This means that God is transforming each one of you into the Holy of Holies, his dwelling*

place, through the power of the Holy Spirit living in you! (Ephesians 2:20-22)

Don't you realize that together you have become God's inner sanctuary and that the Spirit of God makes his permanent home in you? (1 Corinthians 3:16)

So now that you are thinking more about men than music and buildings, union with Jesus and the vital relationships He has established among His people become paramount to the rebuilding of this Presence-obsessed tabernacle.

The Necessity
of an Apostle

In March of 2015, I was invited to attend a meeting with Apostle Damon Thompson in which he was going to spend time with several of us young leaders and talk about what God is doing in our day. At that time, I was serving in a ministry but I was totally disconnected from the authority of a true apostle and spiritual father. While I knew the term *spiritual father*, it was after that day I would know that it was much more significant to what God was doing than I could have imagined.

That meeting began with Apostle Damon giving us "Five Necessities of a Burning Man." I know you would love to know all five, but the very first key was enough to change my life forever. I want to now share that piece with you.

The necessity of an apostle. It is non-negotiable, and the best thing you could do, especially if you are a pastor or leader of a local church, is shut everything down until you find one. That's exactly what I did, because we will never see the order of fathers and sons established until that order comes to church leadership first.

That's where I want to start—with the significance of apostles. I don't think we will be able to see legitimate spiritual fathers raising up spiritual sons until leaders in the church are given permission to become more than their titles and recapture the identity of sons and return back to the order of being joined to apostolic fathers within the leadership structure of the church.

More importantly, for you to see God rightly as Abba and to see yourself as a son, it will require you to walk that out with someone in the natural.

May we not make the mistake that David made, expecting two brothers to lead this journey, when it will take sons joined to a father in order to carry His Presence back to its rightful place. Brothers can bring incredible joy into our lives, but fathers have the ability to teach, correct, and send us into our ultimate fulfillment and design within the Kingdom of God. Simply put, brothers cannot do what fathers can.

Accountability in brotherhood is not a complete biblical model. Irreproachable transparency to someone who has the ability to shut you down is God's idea of submission. You can join yourself with one another in order to walk together, but we cannot submit ourselves to one another as brothers alone. We must have fathers!

I realize that this is a subject, position, and title that has been abused over the years, but it does not excuse us from building with the blueprints of the New Testament church.

I know many who have suffered under slave masters because they submitted their lives to "spiritual fathers" who were nothing more than insecure political kings like Saul. Some even perverted and used the terms of home and family to keep people enslaved to their vision, but I will not refuse the New Testament standard of leadership because of a few bad apples in the bunch.

We need apostles and we need fathers!

The order of fathers and sons is so evident in scripture. When God speaks of Himself, He reveals Himself to us as the God of Abraham, Isaac, and Jacob. Beyond just natural succession, there is also spiritual succession like Moses to Joshua or Elijah to Elisha. God honors the order of fathers and sons so much that He felt it was significant for genealogies to be recorded within the writing of the Bible. Even the gospels begin with the order of fathers and sons.

The last prophetic warning of the Old Testament was:

> Behold, I will send you Elijah the prophet before the coming of the great and dreadful day of the Lord. And he will turn the hearts of the fathers to the children, and the hearts of the children to their fathers, lest I come and strike the earth with a curse (Malachi 4:5-6 NKJV).

Following that warning, God let Israel sit in silence for 400 years. Why? There are several reasons; however, I believe it is because the order of fathers and sons must become paramount if we are to properly prepare the earth for the establishment of the Kingdom of God on the earth.

It's time for us to mature and come out from under the government of babysitters. Paul said in 1 Corinthians 4:15:

Although you could have countless babysitters [teachers] *in Christ telling you what you're doing wrong, you don't have many fathers who correct you in love. But I'm a true father to you, for I became your father when I gave you the gospel and brought you into union with Jesus, the Anointed One.*

Just as I announced earlier that brothers cannot do what fathers can, let me assure you that babysitters cannot raise mature sons in the Kingdom either. I use the term *babysitters* because the word *teacher* in 1 Corinthians 4:15 is a Greek word that means "a tutor, a guide and guardian of boys."

We have lived under teachers in the body of Christ for decades in the West—brilliant teachers at that—on television, radio, and now podcasts and online courses. We have access to the Bible and teachers unlike any generation, and yet with all the access we have to babysitters we have not seen true maturity, which would be evidenced by the transformation of culture.

Teaching certainly helps, but listening to something from someone is a lot different than living the lifestyle with the one who brought you the teaching. That's what fathers do. They bring the gospel to you beyond teaching and get involved in the details of your life. They don't care if you can regurgitate the message to your friends or share it with the world on social media. They want to see you walk it out.

Yahweh is dealing with the wineskin of the church in the West and allowing seemingly destructive forces to cripple our institutions so that we can once again open our eyes to the apostolic nature of the early church, which is founded upon relationships. The reformation we are witnessing in its infancy stages now demands we understand and accept the role of apostles and prophets as the foundational pieces of leadership within the church.

In order to embrace these incredible gifts, we must answer the call of the Holy Spirit, who is calling us out of the systems and institutions of man that have kept us from the relational and governmental blueprint of the church Jesus promised to build.

Most are not willing to embrace this blueprint because the cost is much higher. The systems of institutionalized religion require attendance, rituals, and serving in the vision of that house. The order of fathers and sons requires openness, honesty, transparency, vulnerability, and accountability. It is much easier to hide behind a position than sit with a father face to face.

The order of fathers and sons requires you to remove the mask of religion, expose the depths of your own heart, and accept the love, correction, and direction of a father into maturity in Christ.

This order of fathers and sons begins with the restoration of apostles leading the church.

The term *apostle* is not a cool buzzword I'm trying to use for the next great church growth movement. Apostles bring us back to the original intent or the restoration of the apostolic nature of the church.

The word *apostle* is not a religious term. It is actually a naval term that was used during the time of the ancient Greek orator Demosthenes (284–322 BC) to describe an admiral, the fleet of ships that traveled with him, and the specialized crew who accompanied and assisted the admiral.

The mission of the apostle was to locate territories where civilization was either non-existent or not advancing as it should. Once a place was identified, the apostle along with his crew would unload the ships, settle down, and work as a team to establish a community that reflected the nation they were sent from.

This was no small task. The apostle along with his team would take a strange land and begin the process of transforming it into a replica of a life lived as it was in their home nation. Their purpose was total colonization of uncivilized regions.

This concept of the apostle was so important that Paul said in 1 Corinthians 12:27-28:

> You are the body of the Anointed One, and each of you is a unique and vital part of it. God has placed in the church the following: First apostles, second prophets, third teachers, then those with gifts of miracles, gifts of divine healing, gifts of revelation knowledge, gifts of leadership, and gifts of different kinds of tongues.

In a generation constantly crying out for unity, we cannot have unity without the appropriate order in which the church must function. The very first thing God appoints in the church is apostles. He's also not just talking about the apostles whom Jesus called while He walked the earth. He is saying apostles must be continually serving the body of Christ at all times in order for there to be an actual, healthy body of Christ. If you are connected to a local expression of the church whose leadership is not relationally connected to an apostle, you are not building according to the blueprint of God.

For too long we have allowed administrators, businessmen, and teachers to run the church, when the Bible is clear that apostles and prophets are the governing foundation of the church. Apostles must be present in building the new tabernacle of God's Presence. By divine order they must have first place after Christ or the body is not structured properly, and therefore we can't say to the gift of the apostle, "We don't need you." Yet many of you, just like me, grew up in institutionalized churches where the wisdom of men and church traditions had forsaken the divine order of God for building the church.

Take a moment to really look at the verse above and notice where teachers and leaders appear. As it relates to leadership, we are talking about administration, yet that does not appear at the top of the list. The institutional church has pushed out the gifts of the apostles and prophets and, instead of looking to the blueprints of God to build His church, has looked to the needs of the people to be satisfied by teachers and administrators.

Teachers and administrators are not supposed to serve the people according to their needs; they are supposed to serve under the direction of the apostles to determine how God wants to build His church. This is what I call "shepherding the apostolic." My call as a pastor/teacher is to take the apostolic teaching from my apostle and implement it through my gift to shepherd the people.

I never look to the needs of my congregation or current events to determine what I should preach to the kingdom family I lead here in Covington, Georgia. I look to the divine order that has been established in my life by way of connection to my apostle, and when Yahweh trumpets a message through him as my spiritual father, I then take that word into my secret place and allow the

Father to show me how to shepherd His people into apostolic teaching.

Let me be clear—I don't just take his words and preach them word for word. I take the overall emphasis and allow Holy Spirit to show me how to shepherd our people into it. However, that connection between apostles and pastors/teachers is so real that even if I have not heard my apostle teach in some time, the flow of the word of the Lord stays very closely connected, because this divine order is not a strategy—it is spiritual. It is the order of how we are supposed to carry the Presence of God into our cities.

I can't simply move on from the importance of apostles when many people reject the idea of modern-day apostles. This is foolishness. God has not only appointed them first in order of importance, but they are an ongoing grace for every generation.

> And he has generously given each one of us super-natural grace, according to the size of the gift of Christ. This is why he says: "He ascends into the heavenly heights taking his many captured ones with him, and gifts were given to men." He "ascended" means that he returned to heaven, after he had first descended from the heights of heaven, even to the lower regions, namely, the earth. The same one who descended is also the one who ascended above the heights of heaven, in order to begin the restoration and fulfillment of all things. And he has appointed some with grace to be apostles, and some with grace to be prophets, and some with grace to be evangelists, and some with grace to be pastors, and some with grace to be teachers. And their calling is to

nurture and prepare all the holy believers to do their own works of ministry, and as they do this they will enlarge and build up the body of Christ. These grace ministries will function until we all attain oneness into the faith, until we all experience the fullness of what it means to know the Son of God, and finally we become one into a perfect man with the full dimensions of spiritual maturity and fully developed into the abundance of Christ (Ephesians 4:7-13).

In this one passage, we have to recognize that there are more apostles than the original twelve, and we need to understand how long they will be appointed. It is clear that God gives the graces of apostles, prophets, evangelists, and pastors/teachers to lead the church. However, notice when He appointed the apostles in Ephesians 4—it was when He ascended to the right hand of God. That would not be speaking of the original twelve, who were selected three and half years prior.

When Christ ascended, He appointed more apostles. In His ascension, He appointed these grace gifts to represent His headship to the body and, as Ephesians 4:12 says, to equip the saints for their ministry to build up the body of Christ. But you may still be asking, "How long will He appoint apostles?" Look at Ephesians 4:13—Paul uses the word *until*. Until what?

*These grace ministries will function **until** we all attain oneness into the faith, until we all experience the fullness of what it means to know the Son of God, and finally we become one into a perfect man with the full dimensions of spiritual maturity and fully developed into the abundance of Christ (Ephesians 4:13).*

Take a good look at just the church in the West. Do you feel like we have attained oneness in the faith? Have we all experienced the fullness of what it means to the know the Son of God? Have we become a perfect man (plural) with the full dimensions of spiritual maturity, fully developed in the abundance of Christ? Not quite!

Until has very powerful and generational implications connected to it. All of the things mentioned above cannot be experienced without the grace gifts appointed and currently functioning within the body of Christ.

We must have apostles! Without them, we cannot come to maturity.

When apostles take their rightful place in governing the church, we will then come out from under the entertainment of babysitters and learn to be joined to fathers.

Apostles, like Paul, will help the church understand the order of fathers and sons. You can see that plainly in Paul's letter to Corinth. His rebuke was that they had many teachers, yet they lacked fathers. Not all fathers are apostles, but when apostles are restored, we as the church will once again recognize the importance of fathers to our maturity.

Fathers are more than teachers—they are examples worth imitating. They have a lifestyle and pace to their life worth following. We need men like Paul who can look at a generation of sons and say, "Follow me, as I follow Christ." It is essential if we are to become the bearers of the Presence of God.

This new reformation has begun, and it's not principally a reform of doctrine but rather a reformation of the wineskin and structure of the church. For years we have gathered around doctrine, and all that created was division. But when the church starts gathering around apostles and fathers, the power of the dead, institutionalized church will be broken off of people's lives and a generation will return to the original blueprint of a relational body.

How do I know this is happening? Simple. The fruit of my personal connection to my apostle and spiritual father. But I would go a step further and say the proof is in the connection of my spiritual brothers and sisters to my apostle and spiritual father. I have brothers and sisters leading kingdom families all across the nation and into Canada. Although geography puts distance between us, the apostolic grace that we receive brings us vitally close.

We are no longer scattered, but the grace of an apostle calling us into the life of devotion to Jesus keeps us united. Competition no longer exists; every gift and grace among our kingdom family is recognized and celebrated. When one kingdom family wins, we all share in their victory, and when one family suffers we all feel the impact. We are vitally joined to one another. That does not exist without the order of fathers and sons.

David knew if the Presence of God was going to be restored, he needed the order of fathers and sons to carry it back to Jerusalem. Today, it is no different. The blueprint remains—if we are going to carry His Presence we must follow the blueprint.

If the present gift of apostles and fathers is excluded from our walk, we can never expect to be built together into a habitation for God in the Spirit (see Eph. 2:19-22). We must receive these gifts placed inside of men. When we do, we are receiving Christ. That is not something I made up; this is how Jesus sees it.

In sending out His twelve, He explained to them in Matthew 10:40-41:

> Whoever receives you receives me, and whoever receives me receives the One who sent me. Whoever receives a prophet because he is God's messenger will share a prophet's reward. And whoever welcomes a righteous person because he follows me will also share in his reward.

For all those who say we need to be careful following men, Jesus promises a reward for receiving His grace gifts to us that are in men. Why else would Paul encourage us to submit to them, to each other, as we would submit to Christ? (See Ephesians 5:21.)

Today, our fear of following fathers is the dying groan of an institutionalized system that was careful to follow man, rejecting the notion that what men built was completely structured by their own traditions and not led by God. There is nothing cultish or weird about following the apostolic blueprint of the church Jesus is building. It is built upon following men with evident graces, gifts, and anointings that are further expressions of Christ and should lead you into deeper union with Jesus.

Some will try and challenge this kind of biblical teaching because it simply threatens their independence. However, Jesus has not called us to independence; He has called us into oneness. You are being built together for such a time as this!

This one truth being reclaimed has powerful implications for the days ahead. It becomes our permission to see the apostolic nature and power of the church restored to a world deeply divided. The world needs the fruit of the early church, and many of us pray for it each day. However, we are in error to ask for the fruit of the early church while denying the way in which they ordered their lives.

We must be joined. *Joined* is a New Testament word. Ephesians 4:16 speaks of the body of Christ, "from whom the whole body, joined and knit together by what every joint supplies" (NKJV), or:

> *For his "body" has been formed in his image and is closely joined together and constantly connected as one. And every member has been given divine gifts to contribute to the growth of all; and as these gifts operate effectively throughout the whole body, we are built up and made perfect in love* (Ephesians 4:16).

To be joined is "to fit or frame together (parts of a building, members of a family)." This comes from the Greek root word *syn* denoting union, companionship, association, process, including completeness.

This doesn't happen through strategy and planning community events. This type of joining among Kingdom people must be birthed out of relationship to Jesus. My friend Bobby Lemley says, "Communion reveals community." And we will only enjoy the full benefits of being joined to each other to the level in which we are joined to Christ. He is the foundation of all biblical relationships.

It's time for Abraham, Isaac, and Jacob to walk together again. May Moses provide a space for Joshua to linger in the Presence of God. It's time for Elijah to cast his mantle on another generation of Elishas—not for an altar call, but as an invitation to follow him into a double portion.

If we are going to see the Presence of God properly carried back into our cities, we must commit to walking with fathers in a way that encourages exclusivity to the Lord and a deep love for one another. If your relationship to a father doesn't produce that fruit, find another one.

Today, if I were you, I would be asking for God to reveal to you a spiritual father. If you are a leader, don't plan another Sunday gathering for the church until you ask God to reveal to you where your apostle is. We must be joined to their lives and submitted to their care.

They don't have to be famous, gifted, or talented. They just need to have an evident apostolic grace and a life worth imitating in Christ. Don't look for the well known; find the one who walks with God, has remained faithful to his wife, and has raised godly offspring.

Also let me add, spiritual fathers don't chase sons; sons are to pursue fathers. Some have told me over the years that Jesus leaves the ninety-nine and goes after the one. Yet they forget in that particular story that the lamb was once a part of the ninety-nine. The one that wandered at one time was joined.

There are times when fathers come looking for the one, but also look at the story of the prodigal son or, as my apostle calls it, the story of the redeemed heir. A good father also knows how to patiently wait for a son to come home. It is up to you to come home.

Like Elisha, you must recognize when your Elijah passes by and places his mantle on your life. Elijah said nothing to him after their initial encounter because it was up to the spiritual son to make the decision to slay the oxen, burn the plow, and run after Elijah.

This is not just a word for men, but I'm speaking to some Ruths who need to stay vitally connected to their Naomi. Ruth lost everything, and all she had was her mother-in-law who lost everything too. However, Ruth made a decision to stay joined to her spiritual mother. It was her honor and connection to Naomi that helped position her from gleaning on the corners like the poor, to becoming a deed holder of the field.

That kind of reward I speak of when I talk about Joshua, Elisha, and Ruth will require something deeper than attending a church. You have to get joined to the same level these people did to their spiritual fathers and mothers. You will have to do life together.

If you find yourself reading this book and know you are not connected to a church that has a personal connection to an apostle, or you are not connected to a father, don't cause a stink where you are. In honor, transition and find a place where they are at least relationally joined and connected to the grace of apostles. Then watch that grace come upon your life. The fruit will be undeniable.

It has been true for me. In 2015, I left what some would call a very successful ministry to find my apostle. Although our ministry had exploded numerically and opportunities were endless, it was not scratching the itch for biblical Christianity. I knew there was a grace deeper than my gifting and ability to entertain church people. I knew there was a grace that could help my anxious mind and tired body find my home in Christ. But it didn't happen until I was willing to walk away from what people call "success" to find the grace present within the joining of an apostle and spiritual father.

People thought I was crazy, including some of my own family. I was accused of backsliding, neglecting my call, letting a generation go to hell, and joining a cult. Yet God would allow those lies to be swallowed up in the grace of being properly aligned.

We moved to a little town in South Carolina to be joined to a man we deeply trusted as someone I knew was truly following Christ. He had been identified as one with the grace of apostleship and was someone who had always carried the word of the Lord for my wife and me throughout the years.

In a small town, in a small church, away from ministerial success, God took me on a journey of recovering my true self. That would not have been possible without a spiritual father in my life who cared more about my heart and family than the success of my ministry. That was not possible without an apostle who was able to break free from the system himself and give people permission to place Jesus back at the center of our lives. He did not care about my ministry as much as the actual condition of my heart, and it has made all the difference in me as a man, husband, and father.

Suddenly, anxiety was replaced by peace, isolation was swallowed up in the family, and ministry became an overflow from devotion, instead of another performance on the treadmill of religion.

I didn't have much to show those who wanted to know about my ministry. However, those who actually cared about me got to watch me become a son resurrected in the life of Christ. Today we stand confidently in Christ knowing that we were sent by an apostle to plant the church we lead today.

We are three years into planting our lives in Covington, Georgia, and when people call to check on me, they expect to hear the struggles of a church planter. Instead, they are left in awe of Abba's grace, provision, and direction. I want to say, without a doubt, that the grace we have walked in planting our lives in Georgia has not come by way of our gifts, talents, or abilities. It's because we have built according to God's blueprint of being joined to an apostle and submitted to a spiritual father.

I've got a question—have you ever been thirsty and walked up to a vending machine full of drinks, put your money in, and made your selection only to see the machine type out the words *out of order* on the screen? It is incredibly disappointing. And yet today, many are searching, looking for the fruit of the New Testament in our current expression of the church, and have left disappointed because we have lacked the power and authority that the scriptures say we can experience. We too are out of order.

But Abba is restoring His Presence through the order of fathers and sons, and in those places you will begin to see the apostolic grace and fruit of the church present again.

I hope that you and many others reading this book begin to thirst for a true New Testament expression of the church. It's our only hope for restoring God's Presence in our cities.

A Word for Shepherds

In an hour when the apostolic and prophetic are being restored to their rightful place in the church, many are making the mistake of diminishing the role of a shepherd. However, the function of true apostles does not reduce but rather enhances the role of shepherding within the ekklesia.

We must allow the Holy Spirit to help us redefine this grace gifting within the church back to its original intent. We must move beyond the systemic paradigms of denominationalism's definition of the busy pastor and once again recapture the heart of the shepherd boy in Bethlehem. Although he was never entirely accepted by his own family and was rejected by King Saul, this shepherd boy with a harp and slingshot found his way to the throne.

The shepherd's work is not valued in a day in which we have embraced a conference model, highlighting gifted communicators to astonish crowds with their fresh insight. This model has taught a generation to live off the thrills of Christian entertainment rather than being planted in an Acts church community of family that gathers around the Presence of God, is equipped by fathers, and is called to live their life rooted in devotion to Jesus daily.

No wonder the role of the shepherd is so devalued among leaders. Who wants to be the person who gives their life to one city, one people, day in and day out? Who wants to get their hands dirty among the flock when they could work their craft of preaching, travel, and be featured on the conference poster without the personal responsibility to raise sons? This conference model has promoted an ambitious culture that thrives off man's applause, causing many leaders to exchange the humility of shepherds like David for the flashy armor of a political king like Saul. One produced a legacy that will last forever, while the other had a life of torment struggling to enhance his personal destiny.

My story is one that was called from the flashiness of conference Christianity to take a journey back to my original intent, in hopes of seeing the apostolic nature of the church restored. For nearly ten years, I traveled our nation, preaching 42 weekends out of the year while being given the title of "pastor" in a ministry-centered model driven by conferences. The excitement of gathering people, hosting meetings, and experiencing the anointing of God caused people to move to be a part of it.

The flock that gathered initially was excited to be there and play their part as a volunteer. But eventually, the wear and tear of being the driving force of services took a toll, and needs began to emerge. There was a cry among people who couldn't be satisfied with the conference messages or by giving them a position to serve. It was the cry for a father, a pastor, to be joined to a family and experience revival.

How could I help when my title was a mockery of the actual function? Because of my extensive travel itinerary and having a wife and three children, my office time existed to prepare messages for the people. I had no time to share my life, only to share sermons honestly. Knowing the need for a shepherd but only being valued as a preacher created a prison around my original intent, which ultimately robbed the people of authentic biblical community.

I blame no one for this struggle; we were doing what the system had taught us to do. However, the internal conflict it caused me took a toll on my physical and mental health, not to mention that I had to stare into the faces of people who knew that even though we saw growth, something was wrong with the wineskin.

How do you shepherd people you don't have time to be with? How do you effectively shepherd without being joined to the proper government of an apostle? None of these issues are solved by programs and systems, but rather by asking Holy Spirit to realign the hearts of true shepherds to see the Presence of God restored to our churches and cities.

Someone will have to reject the flashiness of Saul's personality cult to see shepherd-kings positioned to restore the Presence of God to our cities. Apostles help you do that.

There is only one shepherd I can find mentioned or at least named during the reign of King Saul. First Samuel 21:7 says, "Now one of Saul's servants was there that day, detained before the Lord; he was Doeg the Edomite, Saul's chief shepherd" (NIV). *Doeg* in Hebrew means "fearful," from the root word *da'ag* meaning "to fear, be anxious, be concerned, be afraid, be careful, sorrow, take thought."

His name is literally the antithesis of Paul's admonition to be "anxious for nothing" and Jesus' words "take no thought for tomorrow." The system of politics will always put you at odds with the promises of the Kingdom.

Shepherds will always operate in fear while under the institutionalized leadership of political systems and denominations. They are rated on their performance, forced to file performance reports, and encouraged to produce more rather than fathered into their identity, which produces greatness effortlessly.

However, there was another priest present during this time, named Abiathar, who was able to escape the political leadership of King Saul. When he found David—David who was the true, beloved king—he promised to protect him. Interestingly enough, Abiathar's name means "father of abundance" or "my father is great."

When you are under the leadership of politics, you will always live in the fear of failure, constantly running on the treadmill of performance, but when you get joined to actual fathers, you will become a man who doesn't worry about performance, because he knows he is protected by a beloved King of abundance. The same is true when you are joined to apostles and fathers.

I want to share a word of prophecy with you that was given on December 30, 2016 by Apostle Damon Thompson, which I titled "Shepherds on Fire."

You will see in 2017 the most extreme resurrection of pastoral authority in the history of the church. Shepherds are going to get breathed on this year in a way religion told us only apostles and prophets could be used. You're going to see men who smell like sheep begin to wipe out tumors this year. There is something royal coming to the shepherds this year. Many pastors allowed themselves to be called apostles and prophets because they didn't want to care for people, but

I want to rescue the title "pastor" from third, fourth, or fifth down the rung of an illegitimate understanding of authority. You're going to see the hand of God come upon the shepherds this year. And they're not going to have to bring in guest speakers to have a move of God. They are going to start having a move of God on Wednesday nights as they get up to teach Bible study. And the way their people perceive them is going to shift this year. The perception of the people as it relates to the authority of leaders is going to begin to shift like we've never seen before. Some of you who have rejected the shepherd title because of all the sheep dung that comes with it are going to find legitimate fathers who will give you permission to function as biblical pastors rather than systemic ones. That pastor thing is going to start to come alive on the inside of some people who have identified themselves as evangelistic because they are unwilling to sit still. I'm going to send some sons not just to start fires—I'm going to send them to start homes.

I have personally witnessed this transformation in many of my brothers and sisters who are pastoring around the nation. May this word help shepherds find their true fire, but also give you a small window into how powerful the voice of an apostle can be in the life of a shepherd.

God is using the apostolic to identify these shepherds on fire. Let it be said of you as it was David, "I took you from tending sheep in the pasture and selected you to be the leader of my people Israel" (2 Sam. 7:8 NLT). Many of you reading this today are going to see a fresh fire restored to you that the cares of the sheep and the absence of a father once quenched. As you say yes to finding your apostle and father, it will provide grace for a fresh flame on the altar of your life. You will stop striving to build the church Jesus promised to build, and you will start raising the family of God.

Also, the quicker we stop trying to build the church, the quicker we will bring maturity to the sons. This is a lesson I learned early when I came to Covington, Georgia to establish what we call an apostolic revival culture. The Lord said to me, "Mark, I did not send you here to plant a church. I sent you here to get men planted."

It's priceless. Find your apostle. Get roots. it will make all the difference in your life.

A Presence-Obsessed People

At the beginning of 2015, we hosted a gathering of thousands of believers in Cleveland, Tennessee, and we watched the absolute Presence of God wreck our lives. We entered into a time of ecstatic worship, and in the joy of the moment, I remembered that behind the stage we had a life-sized styrofoam replica of the Ark of the Covenant.

I asked my friend and worship leader, Chris Burns, to join me along with two other musicians, and we completely demolished the set on stage in order to make room for the Ark to be brought out. When we brought it out, young people from all over the auditorium gathered and began to dance violently around the Ark.

This caused an absolute firestorm on the internet because people with no spiritual discernment could recognize the prophetic significance of that moment. We all knew we weren't dancing around the literal Ark of the Covenant, but it was a prophetic act calling a generation into a new day of hosting His Presence.

After that night, I called the ministry we were leading at the time into 40 days of hosting the Presence of God nightly at our building. It was a glorious time of intimacy, tears, passion, and anticipation for what God was about to do in our lives. After several nights of gathering and making Abba's Presence the priority, I heard the voice of God say, "This is forty days for forty years. A time to plant the seeds for the greatest reformation in church history."

At the end of those forty days, I was preaching my usual Saturday morning session at our largest youth event that we hosted every year. Right there in front of 5,000 screaming teenagers, the Lord interrupted my message and started talking to me. He said, "The spirit of 1776 has come upon this generation. Just as your forefathers cast off the yoke of the tyranny of Great Britain, so shall this generation cast off the yoke of the tyranny of religion and come into the glorious liberty of being the sons and daughters of Yahweh. And if you want to be a part of it, you will be required to make revolutionary decisions."

That month was the beginning of what my apostle calls "systemic exodus." That was my Nacon's threshing floor moment when I realized the current wineskin of the church, no matter how "successful" man deemed it to be, was not scratching the itch in my heart as a man who longed for the Presence of God.

This book is not being written by a man who has not experienced ministerial success, sitting in the bleachers pointing my finger in jealousy at "successful" people. I know what it's like to see a small beginning of six people become thousands. I have watched millions of dollars come in and been a part of watching a 23-million dollar facility be erected, debt-free, five months before we had the first service.

For almost a decade, I traveled forty-two weekends out of the year, was featured on Christian television, preached at conferences, and knew how it felt to be the honored guest in church houses all over this country. I preached for some of my heroes and shared the stage with amazing worship artists, but in that moment of realizing there was a revolution on the horizon, none of what I was raised to call ministerial success mattered. I knew God was doing something new, and I had to be a part of it.

When Abba interrupted my message that day, I had to admit that I was the one yoked to religion and stuck on the treadmill of performance. I had to admit that my pace was off from the way of Jesus. I had to have enough humility to admit that I had traded my Presence obsession for ministry success.

To the surprise of many, I resigned from the ministry I helped birth. I didn't know exactly what was next, but I could not let this revolutionary moment pass me by because of the opinions of others. My decision to resign led to Abba asking me to shut down my full itinerary and do the very things that I have written to you in the pages of this book.

I walked away from it all because I heard a frequency in the voice of Damon Thompson calling us out of the dysfunctional model of conference Christianity. At that moment, I could have given you a thousand reasons why I needed to walk away, but years later I recognize there is really only one reason—He was jealous for me. He wanted me locked back into the face-to-face gaze of His furious love.

This story of David's journey to restore the Presence of God is my story and the story of many others who were stuck in this modern-day church system. I may be just a few steps ahead of others in the journey; however, I know He brought me out of systemic religion early so I could help others find their way back, under the weight of His glory, to find the way of glory again!

Just as David discovered the way to carry His Presence, the Lord supernaturally led me on a journey as well. He gave me a certain father and a certain family. I found my Levites from the house of Kohath who could get up under the weight of God's Presence and see it rearrange my whole world.

That decision to walk away from everything that I knew in systemic religion not only brought me back to face-to-face encounters with Jesus, but my wife and children began to come alive with things that I never knew existed in them. My whole house became rich in the Presence of God. My children were encountering Jesus in supernatural ways, and we experienced supernatural provision the entire time we said yes to living this life exclusively unto Jesus.

As a matter of fact, the very week I laid my full itinerary down at the feet of Jesus, God moved upon the heart of a businessman to call and see what I needed. I half-jokingly said to the man, "I need a salary."

His reply was, "That's exactly why I am calling you." The Lord had shown this businessman that He had brought me into this new place in life in order for me to sit still, for what would become three years, and to inherit the Kingdom blueprints for a new expression coming into the earth that we now call *apostolic revival cultures.*

Yes, walking away from everything you know is a *huge* risk, not to mention that no one could comprehend that someone would walk away from "success" in ministry to just be with Jesus. So we had to endure the rumor mill, accusations, and warnings from religious leaders who just couldn't accept that our only reason for leaving was because we wanted more of *Jesus.* We were accused of neglecting our call and letting a generation go to hell while I "rested" in the wilderness. Let's not leave out that some accused us of joining a cult.

Who knew that we would be persecuted for choosing Jesus, being captivated by the gospel, and becoming a living witness among our community? I didn't realize that saying yes to the life of devotion without a microphone and a platform could be so controversial.

So let me just go ahead and warn you. When you walk away to inherit the protocol for this new day, don't expect everyone to throw a party because you want the real thing. Some just cannot and will not understand why or when God starts doing something new.

It wasn't long after my transition in 2015 that the Lord gave me a vision that I believe is important for those of you today looking for the next step.

In February of 2016, I had a vision. I saw three men, all recognized by many as apostles in the church today, sitting on a platform. Above their heads were blue portals, which I knew were open heavens, and lightning strikes were producing something in their hands. As it began to unfold, I saw that these lightning strikes produce blueprints for the church. I knew radical changes were to be announced to the remnant.

So I asked the Lord, "How do I stay in step with what You are doing?" Immediately He took me back to an aerial view of this gathering and showed me a new generation sitting on the floor in a childlike position. His response to me was crystal clear. "It looks like children sitting at My feet."

Since that word came, I have been meditating and writing from this whisper, and I want to begin preparing those who will listen for the radical shift that is happening. I do not know what it all looks like; I just want to share my part. I see many voices from the triumphant remnant that will come forward in the days ahead, sharing more pieces of the puzzle and how to posture ourselves to receive the new thing the Lord is doing.

In Mark 10:13-16, we see a beautiful picture of what I believe is a key for the days ahead:

> *The parents kept bringing their little children to Jesus so that he would lay his hands on them and bless them. But the disciples kept rebuking and scolding the people for doing it. When Jesus saw what was happening, he became indignant with his disciples and said to them, "Let all the little children come to me and never hinder them! Don't you know that God's kingdom exists for such as these? Listen to the truth I speak: Whoever does not open their arms to receive God's kingdom like a teachable child will never enter it." Then he embraced each child, and laying his hands on them, he lovingly blessed each one* (Mark 10:13-16).

We must become like a teachable child. We cannot allow religious notions from previous systems and seasons to be the lens of interpretation for what the Holy Spirit is showing us by revelation today. I am not saying the Bible is not a primary source of guidance; what I am warning is that you don't allow a religious, traditional, or even denominational interpretation of scripture to keep you from what the Holy Spirit is revealing this day.

The religious spirit will try to exalt man's traditions to the same authority as God's Word. It is from this exaltation of tradition that we become hardened to change and fight against the truth. The same spirit of religion that has fought against Elijah, Jeremiah, John the Baptist, Jesus, and Paul still exists today, and we must be prepared to stand our ground.

In the 1500s, Martin Luther was considered a troubled soul, an apostate, author of the Great Apostasy, and corrupter of the church. We now call him the great Reformer. In the 1700s, George Whitfield was shunned by most churches and was forced to preach in fields because he didn't fit the common church traditions. These two men are now considered heroes in church history.

How many times have we forced the truth out of the church because we refuse to change? We cannot be know-it-alls. We must be willing to embrace mystery with childlike wonder and simple trust that Abba is leading us. If we ask for bread, will He give us a stone? We also cannot act like what God is saying is not for us.

The book of Revelation tells us that John was caught up in the Spirit on the Lord's Day and heard a voice call from behind. I believe it is possible to walk closely with the Lord and still be turned the wrong way. This keeps us humble, never reaching a place of stagnation in the journey, feeling we don't have to listen for a new word of direction. If we are honest, most of what we call maturity in the church today is passionless intellect posing as an intimate pursuit.

Jesus spoke of the religious when He said, "You search the Scriptures because you think they give you eternal life. But the Scriptures point to me!" (John 5:39 NLT). If scripture does not lead to an encounter with Jesus, you are on the path to becoming the same religious individuals who missed the Messiah when He was standing in front of them. Don't allow yourself to be found in this company. These are the people Jesus called, hypocrites, evil, adulterous, serpents, generation of vipers, fools, blind guides, and whitewashed tombs full of dead men's bones. The only way to keep out of that company is to repent from all *false* forms of religious maturity in order to embrace what is upon us.

The people who were hindering the little children in Mark 10 were His disciples. The greatest enemies we will face, keeping us out of the lap of Jesus, are those posing as the religiously mature. I mean no disrespect, but the majority of leaders in the current church system will be the ones who will oppose what the child-like find in the lap of Jesus. What made the disciples rebuke the children and try to keep them away? It was false requirements established by the religious notion that children were not a worthy use of time for the Messiah.

Surely the Messiah does not have time for such childish behavior. This type of thinking is what has produced many self-righteous members in the church but very few sons who walk in Kingdom authority. Jesus quickly rebukes the actions of His disciples. There is no other place Jesus would have you be than pursuing a seat in His lap. He has no greater desire than to bless His children. But I would be wrong not to mention that when you seek Jesus with a one-thing focus, you will begin to see past the fake, phony, and false.

People will try to talk you out of the pursuit because it rocks the boat of religion and exposes personal compromise. But you keep moving forward and let Jesus handle His leaders. Some may ask, "Why would they keep you away from intimacy with Jesus?"

Well, just like the Reformation with Martin Luther, your intimacy with Jesus might expose the fact that what they are doing in the church is not biblical; it will affect their traditions and practices. For some, it will impact their book sales and ministry following. I wish nothing but goodwill for every son and daughter of Yahweh, but some of these things we are doing in the name of "ministry" are based on either ambition, ignorance, or tradition—certainly not in the truth.

Just imagine for a moment if Peter and those in Acts would have been critical of every detail they were experiencing in the new day of the outpouring of the Holy Spirit? Where was the scripture for fire dancing on their heads? Where was the scripture for speaking in other known languages, diverse tongues? Where was the scripture that permitted their shadows to heal the sick? I'm not saying to throw out discernment, but I am calling you out of being critical of everything that doesn't fit your box.

Jesus said to His disciples in Mark 10:14-15, "Let all the little children come to me and never hinder them! ...Whoever does not open their arms to receive God's kingdom like a teachable child will never enter it." I am asking every one of you reading this book to posture your heart like a teachable child. Come humbly and expect God to reveal new things. It's not new; it's just new to this generation that only knows the current religious church system!

Sitting at His feet is going to play a vital part in bringing forth this revolution in the church. It was the protocol of the Levites when they were given the amazing assignment to carry the Ark of God's Presence. If you are to carry it, you must remain under it and walk in step with those in the family of God who have made the same commitment.

Here's the beautiful thing. In 1 Chronicles 15:26, the Levites David commissioned to carry the Ark found out that if you will position yourself under the weight of His Presence, you won't have to struggle in your assumption that you must carry Him—He will start to carry you. I really believe this is the only way to truly walk into this new day—He will have to carry you there.

So take a deep breath—you don't have to figure it all out. Just sit at His feet, stay under the weight of His glory, and watch Him carry you into a new blueprint for this day.

Those who will make the commitment to stay at His feet will eventually be those who help raise up houses in the order of fathers and sons to give a generation permission to become Presence-obsessed people whose hearts remain set on Him!

I got to witness this with my very own eyes. After leaving everything behind in 2015, we joined ourselves to our spiritual father, Damon Thompson, who at the time was leading a small congregation in the literal wilderness of South Carolina. There beside a stinky chicken processing plant, in the middle of the woods by the country road, with no sign visible, sat a small, white-steepled building we called Hope Chapel.

God began gathering people from all over the country to rearrange their whole worlds to come to the middle of nowhere and make their lives revolve around the Presence of Jesus. The result was tumors vanishing, cancer being healed, and people being delivered by hugs, not to mention guys like me who were absolutely burnt out from the ministry treadmill finding the flame of revival again.

There was no strategy for church growth, just putting Jesus in the center.

We did not plan community-building events; our relationships were forged in the furnace of encounters.

There was no strategic plan for children's ministry because our facilities were so small, and the kids we had just sat in the sanctuary with us. Parents packed snack bags, ipads, and headphones for their kids to sit through four- to five-hour services. When God would settle into that space, kids would put their electronics away and find themselves weeping in the Presence of Jesus.

We didn't have setlists or click tracks, but we made space for musicians to find the Spirit's flow and gave grace to singers to hear the song of the Lord instead of what people heard on Christian radio stations. We didn't have a worship team and an audience; we were all the worshipers with a sound and permission to break our box in worship.

Every Sunday our leadership team of sons would come together, like the early church, and one would have a song, another would have an exhortation, and there was a beautiful symphony of authenticity that flowed between the mutual honor shared among the elders.

This was my introduction to a return to orthodoxy, away from the one-man personality cult, and I was watching the emergence of an Antioch family rising in the earth to redefine the local expression of the church.

I found out in the middle of the woods that people would be willing to lay everything down and move to the middle of nowhere, not because we had incredible discipleship programs, amazing kids' facilities, or we played everyone's favorite worship tune. No, we made Jesus the central focal point and a lifestyle was birthed that many of us didn't even believe was possible in the West.

I say all of that to remind you—Jesus is enough. His Presence is enough, and if we could put all the things we call the church in the peripheral and believe Jesus is enough, there will be a revolution in the church. More importantly, the Presence of God will take preeminence in the land again!

Set Your Heart on Him

"Suddenly a man appeared who was sent from God, a messenger named John. For he came as a witness, to point the way to the Light of Life, and to help everyone believe" (John 1:6-7). John was a man with the pedigree to become something great in Israel, and yet he was given a word that would cause him to leave the temple to embrace the lonely wilderness.

When it came time for a complete reformation of Israel, God first had to call men out of what was, to embrace what was next. John was a man who embraced that call.

John had to disconnect from the predominant religious culture of his day in order to be prepared for the new that was coming, and the same will be true for you. However, this is not a call to deconstruction, where we point at the flaws of a broken systemic church and become isolated from a local assembly. This is a call to disconnect from the traditions of dead Western religious ideology so you can clearly see the One whom you are called to gaze upon.

Apostle John the Beloved wrote, "John announced the truth about him when he taught the people, 'He's the One!'" (John 1:15).

This is the entire key to the Presence movement coming to the globe. A generation is being asked to come out of the dead, dry traditions of man-made religious ideology in the West, which have caused us to see God as the church we created, instead of God as seen in the perfect expression of the life of Jesus. When we set our hearts on Him, it's going to change the entire way we see the church.

Of course, it's hard to raise houses up all over the globe led by the order of fathers and sons, because we have forgotten that our God is a Father and Son dancing together in perfect unity of the Spirit in the timeless dimension.

The church in the West is without the true, tangible Presence of God because we have lost the image of God by setting our hearts on everything but the face of Jesus.

This Presence movement coming to the earth is not about music; it's about the sons of God being restored back to the face-to-face relationship that Adam had before the sin of man brought the grand delusion of separation from God.

A.W. Tozer said that what comes into our mind when we think about God is the most important thing about us. How true a statement that is. We have lost the way of glory because we have lost the glorious image of Jesus.

However, I see a generation of people who are going to commit their entire lives to allow their hearts to remain set on the image of Jesus. Those people who make their lives about one thing will begin to manifest a community of people filled with *zoe* life. *Zoe* is the God-kind of life. That life will become so evident that it will manifest a luminescent lifestyle that the world will not be able to ignore.

Deuteronomy 30:6 speaks of us returning to the Lord, and when we do, the promise is, "The Lord your God will change your heart and the hearts of all your descendants, so that you will love him with all your heart and soul and so you may live!" (NLT).

What an incredible promise for those who will set their hearts on Him! Your heart will be changed. This will not only impact you but will ensure a heart change for your future generations to carry on this covenant love between God and man.

I love this verse because it speaks to a New Testament reality, which is that the Lord changes your heart, but the heart change manifests in a way in which you can truly live! Remember Jesus' words, "A thief has only one thing in mind—he wants to steal, slaughter, and destroy. But I have come to give you everything in abundance, more than you expect—life in its fullness until you overflow!" (John 10:10). I know many religious people in the name of "revival" have told you in times past that Jesus came to show you how to die; however, Jesus makes it very plain that He has come to show you how to live.

The word *live* in Deuteronomy 30:6 is the word *hay*, which means "living, alive; green (of vegetation); flowing, fresh (of water); lively, active (of man); reviving (of the springtime)." It is also a Hebrew word that represents revival and renewal, and it is the word used for community.

Those who turn away from the dead religion of the West to once again place their hearts and eyes on the Person of Jesus are about to manifest a whole new way of life. If your version of revival leads to you becoming more judgmental, critical, constantly finding fault with others, and your services look more like the striving of the prophets of Baal afflicting themselves in order to capture Abba's attention, then you and I are not on the same page.

In an inferior covenant, Moses said that when we turn our hearts to the Lord, our hearts will be changed and we will begin to manifest a life that is like the greenness of fresh vegetation, the flowing of fresh water, lively and active, and reviving like the springtime.

I also believe that we should recognize that the word in Hebrew for revival is the same word for community. You cannot truly be in revival and not be connected to others who are coming alive. An essential part of you moving forward in God is being vitally joined to a family committed to the lifestyle of revival and renewal.

I want to declare over you as the Bridegroom King spoke over the Shulamite in Song of Solomon 2:10-13:

> *Arise, my dearest. Hurry, my darling. Come away with me! I have come as you have asked to draw you to my heart and lead you out. For now is the time, my beautiful one. The season has changed, the bondage of your barren winter has ended, and the season of hiding is over and gone. The rains have soaked the earth and left it bright with blossoming flowers. The season for singing and pruning the vines has arrived. I hear the cooing of doves in our land, filling the air with songs to awaken you and guide you forth. Can you not discern this new day of destiny breaking forth around you? The early signs of my purposes and plans are bursting forth. The budding vines of new life are now blooming everywhere. The fragrance of their flowers whispers, "There is change in the air." Arise, my love, my beautiful companion, and run with me to the higher place. For now is the time to arise and come away with me.*

If you are still reading this book and sense an incredible hunger for more of Him beyond the traditions of man we grew up in and are ready to embrace this day, you first must recognize that you asked Him for this.

He has come just as you have asked. Calling you to His heart will require you to be led out of life as usual. Can you discern this new day and hear Him calling you to a higher place?

He is calling you home. Out of Babylon's idea of church success and back to His original intent. I can hear the words of the Prophet Jeremiah crying out to us today in the West

> "Tell the whole world, and keep nothing back. Raise a signal flag to tell everyone that Babylon will fall! Her images and idols will be shattered.... In those coming days," says the Lord, "the people of Israel will return home together with the people of Judah. They will come weeping and seeking the Lord their God. They will ask the way to Jerusalem and will start back home again. They will bind themselves to the Lord with an eternal covenant that will never be forgotten. My people have been lost sheep. Their shepherds have led them astray and turned them loose in the mountains. They have lost their way and can't remember how to get back to the sheepfold. ...But now, flee from Babylon! Leave the land of the Babylonians. Like male goats at the head of the flock, lead my people home again" (Jeremiah 50:2,4-6,8, NLT).

I recognize this is a prophecy for Israel, but I see a generation currently that is beginning to ask for the way back home, the way back to Jerusalem, which I see as their way back to peace.

For years we have been led by ambitious shepherds who cared for the church more like a business than a family. The results are absolutely devastating. Shepherds lost their way when we started allowing Babylon business principles to guide us into franchise models that we called "church planting."

We sent them into the mountains of influence to change the culture but didn't teach them the way home. So now Abba is calling for leaders in this hour to recognize the error of our ways and become, as Jeremiah said, like a male goat and lead the sons and daughters of God back home to the way of glory!

I believe if you are reading this book, the Lord is calling you to be like the male goat, or ram, which is not easily afraid, will lead without hesitation, and will confidently call others back to the way of the glory! You are being called to the Kingdom for such a time as this!

The pope called Martin Luther a wild boar loose in the vineyard of the Lord. I believe you and I can be the confident ram leading a generation back to the way of the glory. This ram nature comes alive in the hearts of those who begin to follow the path of being absolutely Presence obsessed.

It's the same hunger that drove Charles Finney to climb a mountain and say, "I will give my heart to God, or I will never come down from there."

Hunger caused a businessman named D.L. Moody to write in a journal, "I had got a taste of another world, and cared no more for making money." He got on his knees and cried out, "I don't want to live any longer if I could not have this."

John G. Lake spoke about a man who encountered God and said, "By the end of the year, I believe I was the hungriest man for

God that ever lived. ...It was the yearning passion of my soul, asking for God in a greater measure than I knew. ...My soul was demanding a greater entrance into God, His love, presence, and power."

Lake went on to say following a great encounter, "God, if you will baptize me in the Holy Spirit, and give me the power of God, nothing shall be permitted to stand between me and a hundred-fold obedience."[5]

History shows us that there is always a remnant that, like a ram, will jump out front and lead the charge. Will you be one who allows your hunger to cause you to risk it all for a generation to discover the way of glory again?

There have been many who have started the journey with an absolute Presence obsession but have gotten sidetracked by the supernatural instead of keeping it Jesus focused. We need people who will become so focused on their Presence obsession that they don't get distracted by peripheral things. If it could happen to Peter on the Mount of Transfiguration, it could happen to us all.

I'm sure you know the story of Jesus on the Mount of Transfiguration. In this extraordinary encounter in Matthew 17:1-8, Jesus invited Peter, James, and John to accompany Him for an incredible encounter with the Kingdom of God. Jesus became like the light of the brilliance of the sun, and Moses and Elijah appeared and started up a conversation with Jesus.

Peter, who is for me the most relatable person in scripture, started scheming a plan to build three tabernacles to celebrate the life of Moses, Elijah, and Jesus. But the scripture says:

But while Peter was still speaking, a bright radiant cloud spread over them, enveloping them all. And God's voice suddenly spoke from the cloud, saying, "This is my dearly loved Son, the constant focus of my delight. Listen to him!" (Matthew 17:5)

This is an incredible lesson that we must heed if we are going to see the glory of the Presence of Jesus invade our lives. We cannot do anything for anyone other than what Jesus tells us to do. The Father is not looking for us to place people, the Law, or the prophets on the same level as Jesus.

I've watched men build entire churches and movements off of the encounters of great people—people worth imitating. But at the end of the day, Jesus is building His church, and I see another cloud of glory coming to this generation that is about to interrupt all our plans. And the voice of Abba is going to call us in the midst of extraordinary encounters and remind us that no matter how supernatural the encounter, nothing needs to be built for anyone or anything unless you have heard Jesus say to do it.

We need Marys who, in John 20:11-13, went to visit the tomb of Jesus. While she was there she encountered two incredible angels and she did not get mesmerized by these angelic beings. She just wanted to know where Jesus was. These are the type of people Jesus is looking for in this hour—Jesus obsessed people. Not people focused on signs and wonders—a real Jesus obsessed people.

We cannot afford to make our lives and the church about anything else but Jesus! We cannot get sidetracked by the supernatural or by how great men and women of the past did certain things. We must be focused with our hearts set on Jesus! It's the only way we are going to see a revolution come to this generation!

May we be like Mary and say, "Whatever He tells you to do, just do it."

We Are Standing at a Crossroads

This is what the Lord says: "Stop at the crossroads and look around. Ask for the old, godly way, and walk in it. Travel its path, and you will find rest for your souls" (Jeremiah 6:16 NLT).

In 1916, Robert Frost wrote a narrative poem entitled "The Road Not Taken." There is one line that has absolutely marked my life over the past seven years, and it says, "Two roads diverged in a wood, and I, I took the one less traveled by, and that has made all the difference."

Seven years ago, Abba brought me to a crossroads and asked me to look around. It didn't take long to discover that I needed to ask for the ancient path, not because I knew what it was, but because I knew I needed rest for my soul. I have done my best these past few years to sit at His feet, and what I have learned has been mind-blowing. My whole world has been turned upside down. To be honest, I have had to unlearn more than I think I have learned.

However, the greatest revelation that has been imparted to me the past seven years is that I am loved by God. Sadly, this revelation did not come to me until I had already been behind the pulpit for a decade. I spent many days at home constantly putting myself under the scrutiny of a god that looked more like Zeus than the loving Abba whom Jesus revealed to His disciples. That translated into a successful ministry of traveling the country preaching the bad news of condemnation.

We need to do more, pray more, fast more, repent more.

This type of religious thinking has halted the journey of restoring the Presence for many of us reading this book today because we think it all depends on us. It's true that we need to disconnect from the compromised priesthood, not make the mistakes of the traveling prophets, and refuse to participate in the slavery of political kings. But to reject these inferior positions and not embrace the fullness of our identity in Christ would be a tragedy.

How did David restore the Presence of God to his city after failing miserably at Nacon's threshing floor? Of course, he learned the proper protocol to carrying the Presence of God, but he refused to continue the journey until he knew God was no longer angry. Go back and read the story again.

David was angry because the Lord's anger had burst out against Uzzah. David was now afraid of the Lord, and he asked, "How can I ever bring the Ark of the Lord back into my care?"

Several verses later, nearly three months later, someone told the king, "The Lord has blessed Obed-Edom's household and everything he has because of the Ark of God."

Even though David's name meant "beloved," his identity as one loved by God could not be secure until he knew that God was no longer angry. I would spend more time on the subject of receiving your beloved identity; however, if you still see God as revealed on Mount Sinai, you are going to struggle to believe you could be a part of making history with Him!

For years we have heard prophets declare the "key of David." There are several interpretations, but I believe David's key is knowing that he was loved by God. This is your identity too. David did not just wake up one day to believe that. His identity had been thoroughly tested, whether it was facing the rejection of his father, dealing with the belittlement of his brothers, or even being rejected by his "spiritual father" Saul, David had to believe he was beloved.

Yet David, knowing he was loved, did not continue the journey because he thought God was mad at him. It wasn't until David knew that God was no longer angry that he was able to bring the Presence of God back into Jerusalem.

This tells me that you will never be secure in your identity as one dearly loved—and you will never be able to partner with God in such a significant moment as we are in today—if you still see Him as angry!

I wonder, what measure of His Presence, revelation, and glory are we not walking in currently because we think God is not pleased with us?

This is the crossroads we stand at today. It begins with our idea of who God is and if we will really be willing to accept the pure gospel of Jesus Christ. With the wrong image of God and a distortion of the gospel, we will never be able to see the glory of

God manifest in our lives to the degree Jesus has dreamed for us to experience it.

For years, especially among Pentecostal and Charismatic circles, we have perverted the gospel, mingling grace with the Law, trying to make disciples of Jesus by teaching them Moses, which places us back on the treadmill of performance, teaching us to strive for what Jesus has already provided for us.

Others spent their lives turning the gospel into an intellectual pursuit instead of being intimate with the Bridegroom. They created an idea of God as Western Judge in a courtroom with His gavel in hand, ready to condemn us as sinners. Or, worse, we see Him as Zeus with a thunderbolt ready to strike us down for our mistakes.

No matter how you were raised, we can all agree that Jesus came to the earth to deal with our misconceptions about the Father! Jesus said, "If you have seen Me, you have seen the Father" (John 14:9 VOICE). The writer of Hebrews gave us another window into this revelation when he wrote in Hebrews 1:3, "The Son is the dazzling radiance of God's splendor, the exact expression of God's true nature—his mirror image!"

Are you ready for some good news? This is going to help you take the ancient path. The good news is that God is like Jesus! Jesus is the icon of the invisible God and He is the message of God. As Bill Johnson would say, "Jesus Christ is perfect theology."

Jesus came to articulate clearly what Moses could only see in shadows.

We are not sinners in the hands of an angry God. Jesus spoke to Jewish leaders devoted to the Law of Moses, saying:

My own sheep will hear my voice and I know each one, and they will follow me. I give to them the gift of eternal life and they will never be lost and no one has the power to snatch them out of my hands. My Father, who has given them to me as his gift, is the mightiest of all, and no one has the power to snatch them from my Father's care. The Father and I are one (John 10:27-30).

This is the work Jesus primarily came to do. He wasn't showing us how to die. He was showing us how to live in relationship with the image of the Father revealed in Jesus.

In the most intimate and vulnerable moment, John heard Jesus whisper this prayer to Abba, "Father, I have manifested who you really are and I have revealed you to the men and women that you gave to me" (John 17:6). And in His closing words of that same prayer, Jesus said, "I have revealed to them who you are and I will continue to make you even more real to them, so that they may experience the same endless love that you have for me, for your love will now live in them, even as I live in them!" (John 17:26).

How did Jesus manifest the Father to them? Angry? Frustrated? Critical?

No. As the Happy God who creates more wine to extend the party.

He is the One who accepts the worship of a prostitute and uses her example to teach the religious the proper response to His Presence.

He is the One who protects the adulterous woman from getting stoned, runs off the religious, and doesn't think to condemn her.

So is Jesus defying His Father or exposing the inferior explanation of God found in Moses' description of the shadow of God?

Friend, we are not disciples of Moses, Job, or Jeremiah. We are followers of Jesus who said:

> No one ever before gazed upon the full splendor of God except his uniquely beloved Son, who is cherished by the Father and held close to his heart. Now that he has come to us, he has unfolded the full explanation of who God truly is! (John 1:18)

The good news keeps getting better. Yahweh has chosen to love us with the same love He has for Jesus and has chosen to see us exclusively through the lens of Jesus. Jesus did not come to the earth to make us better rule followers. He came so that we could enjoy the same relationship that He shares with His Father.

When Paul began writing to the church in Rome, he began to expound to them on the role of the Holy Spirit in the life of the believer, saying:

> The mature children of God are those who are moved by the impulses of the Holy Spirit. And you did not receive the "spirit of religious duty," leading you back into the fear of never being good enough. But you have received the "Spirit of full acceptance," enfolding you into the family of God. And you will never feel orphaned, for as he rises up within us, our spirits join him in saying the words of tender affection, "Beloved Father!" For the Holy Spirit makes God's fatherhood

real to us as he whispers into our innermost being,
"You are God's beloved child!" (Romans 8:14-16)

This image of God gives you confidence that nothing is impossible. God is good and you are loved! You can continue the journey knowing the One who has called you to carry His glory loves to be joined to you. You are fully accepted, enfolded into the family of God, and as you take each step, Holy Spirit reminds you, "You are My dearly loved child."

This image of God is the grace to keep you safely in the hands of the potter as you spin wildly on the potter's wheel. This is the God of Jesus who makes all things work together for your good.

The reality of God as Father and our identity as His beloved is what gave my wife and me the grace to leave all that we knew years ago, cancel our itinerary, and watch Abba prove to us that being His son and daughter was enough. During those years, Abba proved to me that He didn't love me for what I did; He loved me because I'm me.

Once you realize that the Presence of God has been restored to you, you will begin to realize how the Presence of God is restored to your city. You are the way of the glory!

Once the Presence of God was restored in David's life, he started tapping into a dimension in God where the New Covenant manifested before the fullness of time came.

Once you realize God is not angry with you, it begins to change the way you see everything. For David, he was able to tap into grace before Jesus ever came to the planet. He had a New Covenant lens before there was a New Covenant.

David started saying things like, "It's not sacrifices that really move your heart. Burnt offerings, sin offerings—those aren't what bring you joy. But when you open my ears and speak to me, I become your willing servant, your prisoner of love for life" (Ps. 40:6).

David said in Psalm 51:16, "For the source of your pleasure is not in my performance or the sacrifices I might offer to you." David was living in a day of an inferior covenant when the religious system of that day said all of those things were required. Yet knowing he was loved allowed him to tap into a revelation that would not be available for generations to come.

Again I ask you the question—what measure of revelation, Presence, and glory are we not walking in currently because we think God is not pleased with us, because we do not realize just how loved we are?

David got even bolder than just talking about the inferior sacrifices of animals being offered when the apostle Paul quoted him in Romans 4:6-8:

> Even King David himself speaks to us regarding the complete wholeness that comes inside a person when God's powerful declaration of righteousness is heard over our life. Apart from our works, God's work is enough. Here's what David says: What happy fulfillment is ahead for those whose rebellion has been forgiven and whose sins are covered by blood. What happy progress comes to them when they hear the Lord speak over them, "I will never hold your sins against you!"

David discovered the revelation of righteousness generations before Paul ever declared the gospel of grace to his generation.

How could he access such profound revelation? The key was David discovered that God was good and that he was loved.

In the days to come, the people who will make the most impact upon the culture will be those established in these two primary revelations: God is good and I am loved!

For me, I feel that the Holy Spirit has brought us to a generational crossroads and we are being asked to take a road less traveled in leaving behind our "sinners in the hands of an angry God" Christianity to embrace the God found in the person of Jesus. As one who has been on this path for over seven years at the publishing of this book, I can testify it truly has made all the difference. I have traveled this path and have truly found rest for my soul.

However, there are many who have not yet made a decision. Yet wisdom is calling to you and me. Can you hear her?

> Can't you hear the voice of Wisdom? From the top of the mountains of influence she speaks into the gateways of the glorious city. At the place where pathways merge, at the entrance of every portal, there she stands, ready to impart understanding, shouting aloud to all who enter, preaching her sermon to those who will listen. "I'm calling to you, sons of Adam, yes, and to you daughters as well. Listen to me and you will be prudent and wise. For even the foolish and feeble can receive an understanding heart that will change their inner being. The meaning of my words will release within you revelation for you to reign in life" (Proverbs 8:1-6).

Wisdom stands at the gate of transition and longs to teach us how to enter into a new place in God. Just look around—people are in transition. Some call it a time of transformation, some call it enlightenment, others deconstruction. I just call it the renewing of our mind. No matter how you word it, we are standing at a crossroads, in a moment when a new age is overtaking the old one.

What is this new age or this road less traveled? I believe the Holy Spirit is calling us into the way of the glory. This path is not a concept or a new strategy for the church; it is the very glory of God in the person of Jesus! Jesus is calling us into the purity of the gospel.

The crossroads we stand at is where religion ends and Christ's new world begins. It's a historic moment. As I prayed about what exactly I am sensing, I kept hearing Holy Spirit say that we are in just as significant a transition in the West as Israel was between the resurrection of Jesus and the destruction of the Temple in Jerusalem in A.D. 70.

For a time Israel was living in a forty-year period of the overlapping of two ages. The resurrection of Jesus initiated a whole new way of life. God had announced the end of the "behind the veil age" of the Law of Moses by completely ripping the curtain in the Holy Place from top to bottom.

Yet despite God announcing the end of Judaism, there was a forty-year period when an obsolete priesthood continued to present unnecessary offerings in a temple where God was no longer present. People still participated, and this obsolete religion continued to move forward as if nothing ever happened. The same was true in the life of David. Saul had the kingdom stripped from him, and David had already been anointed. But there were many years between the beginning of the revolution and the actual manifestation of the new era.

I believe we are in such a significant moment, when we too are being asked to help lead people into a brand-new age with the purity of the gospel despite the religious world continuing in the same fruitless cycles while a revolution is already underway.

Today, we too are living in the overlapping of two ages, and this is far beyond a reformation of the church. This will realign the nations of the world. In one age we have people still bound under the Law of Moses, making revival nothing more than religious self effort and celebrating the destruction of the planet as a sign of the times. And the other age is now overtaking the planet, in which the sons of God are going to manifest because we have the wonder of the gospel restoring the planet.

While many are declaring that these are the last days, I would say they certainly are the last days of the West as we have known it. We are about to experience a global outpouring, and the United States of America is going to have to humbly learn from other nations what the Kingdom of God actually looks like.

Today we need men and women like the apostle Paul to help lead us in this overlapping of two ages. This man was absolutely hand-picked for helping others navigate those tumultuous times in the Middle East.

In his first age, he was known as Saul of Tarsus. In Acts 7:58 we learn about his pre-conversion status. He was a Pharisee, one zealous for the Law, hyper-nationalistic, and was trained under one of the greatest teachers in the history of Israel. Saul was a man with an incredible pedigree both nationally and in his religion.

Saul was born in Tarsus in Cilicia during the days of Rome occupying Judea (see Acts 22:3). Tarsus was a city in good standing with Rome; therefore, Saul was a citizen of Rome. Yet he studied in Jerusalem with Gamaliel. He was born in a tent-making home, which at the time was considered a good trade, so he would have come from a fairly wealthy family.

Although Saul grew up in a Roman-occupied territory, the mind-set of the day was Greek or Hellenistic, which was very creative and sexual. Interestingly enough, Jews, especially ones like Saul, hated Hellenization. So check out the time in which Paul lived—the political realm was Roman, the social mindset was Greek, and Paul wanted to be a Pharisee and participate in a Jewish revolt against the Roman government and Greek culture.

However, being a Roman carried incredible benefits affording Saul the ability to travel uninterrupted anywhere he wanted. Saul would have been considered elite—he couldn't be beaten or tried without due process in a Roman court setting. A city could lose its Roman status over the beating of a Roman.

Yet despite his incredible Roman pedigree, he was also a Hebrew from the tribe of Benjamin. Could you imagine the whirlwind of thoughts running through this young man's mind politically and theologically? He was a Roman citizen, born in a Greek town, and could speak Koine Greek, yet he was passionate about his Hebrew heritage. Jerusalem would have been his deepest concern, and as a Pharisee, he would have believed that all of Israel would have to say yes to God's Law and be fully obedient in order for God to bless the nation. So all other political, cultural, and religious practices must be opposed to their way of life. Israel must be cleansed enough for the Messiah to appear.

Saul would have believed that if the nation would obey completely, the Messiah would come and establish His political throne of David and free Israel from that present evil age. To Saul, Christianity would have been considered a total threat to Judaism, to the nation, and especially to the Pharisees who used the political climate of Rome to their advantage.

This explains why you see Paul at the stoning of Stephen in Acts 7, because he hated Christians and wanted them all to die. He would consider Christians as making their nation unclean and impure, because the nation of Israel must remain the home of the Law and the Torah for the children of Israel to be able to be the people of God.

Paul would have wanted Romans to get out, to drive all Hellenistic thinking out, and to restore the purity of the bloodline of Jews, for full obedience to the Law. If anyone understood Judaism and religion, Saul did! In one of his post-conversion letters, Paul described himself as one who was a true Hebrew, from the tribe of Benjamin, which was the most loyal to the house of David. He was circumcised on the eighth day, raised in the strict tradition of Orthodox Judaism, and lived a separated and devout life as a Pharisee. Concerning the righteousness of the Torah, no one out-performed him. He was a fiery defender of the truth, persecuting Christians with religious zeal.

God took a man deeply committed to the God of Mount Sinai, fully obedient to the Law of Moses, and used him to declare a whole new way to relate to God.

He was a perfect candidate for taking the road less traveled into the purity of the gospel. How much more perfect could his life have been? He was mingled and tossed in a whirlwind of religious, political, and cultural ideas, which is what prepared him to be the greatest witness of conversion the early church had witnessed.

In this hour of overlapping of ages, God is calling for His Pauls to come out of the lifeless marriage of religion and politics to embrace Christ alone. And that is exactly what Paul did. In Philippians 3:7-8, he said:

> Yet all of the accomplishments that I once took credit for, I've now forsaken them and I regard it all as nothing compared to the delight of experiencing Jesus Christ as my Lord! To truly know him meant letting go of everything from my past and throwing all my boasting on the garbage heap. It's all like a pile of manure to me now, so that I may be enriched in the reality of knowing Jesus Christ and embrace him as Lord in all of his greatness.

Paul went on to say:

> My passion is to be consumed with him and not cling to my own "righteousness" based in keeping the written Law. My only "righteousness" will be his, based on the faithfulness of Jesus Christ—the very righteousness that comes from God (Philippians 3:9).

Let me make it very simple. If you are going to follow the way of the glory, you will have to once and for all leave the old age of Moses and the Law behind to follow Jesus into His finished work. We will never see a generation immersed in the glory of God until we can be finished with the mingling of Law and Grace!

The apostle Paul was a man who learned to navigate in the tension of ages and confronted those who were refusing to make the transition and helped others navigate the difficult waters of religious tension.

Just as David went to the Torah to discover the protocol for bringing the Presence back to Jerusalem, today in the New Covenant we must go back to what Jesus has declared in order to properly bring the way of the glory back to this generation.

Paul's answer for his day of living in the overlapping of two ages was to become absolutely obsessed with Jesus and the gospel of His grace! This will be the key for anyone who longs to be a part of restoring the way of the glory back in this day. We must break free as Saul did from the religious system of his day in order to inherit a new identity and become the dwelling place of God in the Spirit.

I want to emphatically say that you cannot be a part of this Presence movement if you are still living under the law, still eating from the tree of the knowledge of good and evil, and are selfishly still living in sin-consciousness. Religion will always keep you occupied in self-focus because if it can keep you focused on yourself, you will never become like Him or show the world that Christ in you is the hope of glory.

We are standing at a crossroads of a new day. You are being called to restore the way of the glory, and it will require taking the road less traveled. Are you willing to take the path of the purity of the gospel until you and the world realize that you are the way of the glory?

You will only be able to say yes if you believe God is good and you are loved!

The Purity of the Gospel Is the Way of the Glory

What is being shaken in this hour is any man-made structure of religion that is keeping you from realizing who you really are in Christ. It's time for the sons of God to arise from under the government of the compromised priesthood, to no longer live as orphans under the lack of fathering within the traveling prophets, and to once and for all be free from the slavery of political leadership within the church.

You are being called to recover the protocol of restoring the Presence of God to your city. Hopefully by now you recognize that you are the sons and daughters of God, the new priesthood, the new Ark of the Covenant, and your life through the finished work of Christ will become the way of the glory of God to invade the cosmos again! It is the purity of the gospel that ensures that we, the ancient gates, are opened wide for the King of Glory to come in.

Just like Paul, we are being called to trumpet the message of the gospel until man is crowned with glory and we are to fill the earth with His image-bearers until the knowledge of the glory of the Lord covers the earth as the waters cover the sea. We cannot stop declaring the absolute scandalous grace of God until the kingdoms of this world become the kingdoms of our God and His Christ.

We, like Paul, must step into the boldness of declaring this gospel because we, like him, fully understand the depths of devastation in religion. We know what it's like to live in the constant condemnation of sin cycles only to be told by religious leaders you need to do more if you want to experience freedom. We know how much effort we put into being miserable in hopes that somehow we made it hurt bad enough that God would pick us for revival. This mingling of law and grace has not produced any significant or sustained outpouring in our day, and it's time for us to admit that.

What we need is not a revival of morals and rule following. We need an awakening to Abba's original intent for our lives that has now been made possible through the finished work of Christ. Once we discover who we are, we will see the culture of heaven begin to invade the earth, and morality will follow. But to put morals before identity is to set an entire generation up for failure.

I'm afraid in our modern-day cultural firestorm, our immediate knee-jerk reaction is to preach rules. However, what if our revival preaching, which has been nothing more than the Law, was actually fueling the moral decline in our nation? We better learn to preach the good news. It's the only answer for this day.

How have we ignored the reality of New Testament teaching? Paul made it clear that righteousness cannot come through keeping the Law (see Gal. 3:21). You cannot be justified by the Law (see Gal. 2:16), because the Law demands perfection (see James

2:10). Even worse, when we preach the Law we give sin power to exist (see 1 Cor. 15:56).

This is why I say our legalistic preaching of the Law and calling it revival is a great tragedy if we are trying to usher in the Presence of God. Just look at Romans 7:5, which says, "When we were merely living natural lives, the law, through defining sin, actually awakened sinful desires within us, which resulted in bearing the fruit of death."

Yet we continue in this New Covenant to define sin, expecting it to lead to deliverance through Jesus. If we want sin to be dealt its death blow, we must preach the fullness of Jesus and how He takes away the sin of the world!

So how long will we falter between two opinions? How long will we try to keep Old Testament revival paradigms when the message of grace preached by the apostle Paul and the early church flipped the world upside down?

We must stand up for the purity of the gospel in this hour. Like Paul in his letters to the churches in the province of Galatia, we too must take a bold stand in establishing this new age of the gospel!

Galatia was a province in what is now known as Southern Turkey. This was not a letter to a local church but to an entire region. The truths in these six powerful chapters are something every believer should spend their lives continually immersing themselves in. The gospel was exploding in the region, miracles were taking place, and lives were being radically changed.

But in came the religious Jews trying to pervert the gospel by trying to make Christianity merge with Judaism. Religion is afraid to take this journey into freedom because religion loves the rules; it loves to keep us in codependence because we would rather have someone tell us what to do than lean into the dynamic relationship of the Holy Spirit.

I've learned over the years that people would rather have rules than an actual relationship with Holy Spirit.

In these six chapters, Paul endeavored to make sure the gospel remained undiluted and uncompromised so that no one was cheated. He saw a future in which the pure gospel would be embodied in these people. Paul looked into the face of religion and cried out, *"No!"*

This gospel cannot be mixed. It is to remain completely pure. It cannot be related to the Old Covenant in the sense that the Old Covenant is based upon works and traditions that have been fulfilled in Christ. It is over and done with! We are now completely in a New Covenant. Paul went on to share that the gospel is not an intellectual assent but the grace given to empower you to live in this new creation life.

Paul saw the finished work of Christ as a new Passover. For years Israel and the world had been living under the bondage of sin and the powers of darkness. They knew that before Christ they had been living in the present evil age but Jesus' finished work brought them into the age to come, although at that moment it seemed as if the ages had overlapped. In one sense they were; it just took a little while for a new day to be actualized. Remember, God declared the evening and the morning to be the first day, which means the new day doesn't begin with Light.

Paul is letting us all know that we have been rescued from this present evil age, and the gospel declares we now live in a very different world, and we should order our lives accordingly. The finished work of Jesus was not about going to heaven, but deliverance from the dark powers that enslaved the world. It was an announcement that the Kingdom of God had truly come and that we would soon learn to see it on earth as it is in heaven.

For those who can dare to believe—welcome to eternal life. Sin has no more power, the accuser has been silenced, and we have been fully redeemed from the curse of the Law.

So hear me clearly—if we are going to see His Presence restored in this hour, we can't take our old ways into this new world.

In that day, it was about leaving the old world of Judaism, with early church fathers being adamant about Christians not participating in old Jewish practices. Ignatius called the practice of Judaism false teaching, saying, "If we are still living in the practice of Judaism, it is an admission that we have failed to receive the gift of grace."

Yet here we are in 2022, thinking that we are going to usher in a new day of the Spirit of God using Old Testament paradigms, totally ignoring the freedom, grace, and empowerment of the pure gospel! The carriers of His Presence will have to walk a different path in the victory of Christ.

I've heard religious people point their fingers at the preachers of righteousness and accuse us of watering down the message with grace. However, it is religion that takes the potency out of the gospel.

I'm done with religion allowing the sons of God to be ruled by the Law of Moses and allowing the accuser to still whisper the lies of condemnation into the ear of the believer. I'm sick of believers living in the fear of judgment, making the gospel seem "almost finished." Worse yet, we have rearmed principalities through our false spiritual warfare teachings and convinced an entire generation to believe that Jesus is going to rapture us off a planet we are called to rule.

It's time for us to embrace the good news! Jesus came to give us more than an afterlife, but to give us life and life more abundantly. His finished work is a complete victory over the realm of darkness, and we have been fully restored back to our original intent as image-bearers to the world around us.

We have been delivered from the treadmill of religious performance, no longer eating from the tree of the knowledge of good and evil. We can now rest in the finished work of Christ and access the tree of life where we will never die. The days of religious modification are over, and now it's time to declare our true identity in Christ. This is your new life—dearly loved, flawless in Yahweh's eyes, with permanent access to marvelous kindness. You have a perfect relationship with God.

How has Romans 6:6 been recorded for 2,000 years and we still believe that as new creations in Christ we still have a sin nature? Your former identity is now and forever deprived of its power, the stronghold of sin is dismantled, and the realm of darkness has been completely stripped of its power. No more religiously managing the sin that Jesus has already removed. You are free, once and for all, from the cycles of destruction with no more failed attempts at pleasing the One who has chosen in Christ to see you as perfect and flawless.

This is the gospel! You in Christ is what the world is standing on tiptoe to see. We have been called for such a time as this to bring order to the chaos of this created world, to once again see the

Garden of God's pleasure expand its borders until the knowledge of the glory of the Lord covers the earth as the waters cover the sea.

We cannot afford to fight against the grace awakening happening in our day. Let them accuse us of preaching scandalous grace, but we all know the fruit of legalism and the true fruit of the gospel. I will take joy over having my intellectual ego stroked by the doctrines of men. We have nothing to prove in Christ. May we dive into the depths of the "in Him" dimension without hindrance, for the Spirit of Grace is calling us to fully receive our inheritance as the sons and daughters of God.

Almost eight years ago, my apostle, Damon Thompson, said, "In the move of the Spirit, identity would be paramount." For years I have pondered that statement, and now I am beginning to see that the degree to which we are willing to accept our beloved identity will determine how much of the inheritance of God Himself will be entrusted to us.

A stone is being placed in Zion! That's the word I heard recently in one of our services here in Covington, Georgia. Isaiah 28:16 says, "Here's what the Lord God says: Behold, I set in Zion a foundation stone, fully tested and proven to be faithful and secure. And written upon this precious cornerstone is this: Those who trust in him will not be shaken." The word *stone* in Isaiah 28:16 is the Hebrew word for "son."

However, when you see this verse referenced in both Romans 9:33 and 1 Peter 2:1-8, you see that this stone has a different effect on people. In Isaiah 28:16, those who put their trust in Him will not be shaken, but in the two New Testament references, it will cause people to stumble.

> *Be careful! I am setting in Zion a stone that will cause people to stumble, a rock of offense that will make them fall, but believers in him will not experience shame* (Romans 9:33).

I share these verses because it illustrates the overlapping of two ages. One group is able to build their lives on the stone and another group will be offended by it, to the point that they will attack those who build their lives on it.

I'm telling you that we are stepping into a new age in church history when God's incredible goodness and mercy are going to be put on full display. People are going to be offended by the goodness of God. The gospel call is going to be released with such power and mercy we haven't seen since the conversion of the apostle Paul.

I think it will be hard for some of us to accept what God is about to do and who He is about to show Himself through. He's going to call some people you don't like, restore people you hate, and display Himself through those you despise.

What is the way of the glory? It's Christ in me. It's Christ's fullness living and being displayed in and through me.

So stay away from what Paul called "those pretending" in his letter to the church in Colossae:

> *Beware that no one distracts you or intimidates you in their attempt to lead you away from Christ's fullness by pretending to be full of wisdom when they're filled with endless arguments of human logic. For they operate*

with humanistic and clouded judgments based on the mindset of this world system, and not the anointed truths of the Anointed One (Colossians 2:8).

Beware of religious pretenders who try to distract you or intimidate you, to try and lead you away from Christ's fullness! Who are these pretenders? Jesus called the Pharisees frauds and pretenders repeatedly throughout Matthew 23. These men tied heavy religious obligations on people's backs but would never try to help ease the person's load—do more!

Pretenders keep people from experiencing heaven's Kingdom realm, which we know is righteousness, peace, and joy in the Holy Ghost. Pretenders are always killjoys, robbing people of peace, and forbidding people to ever believe they are the righteousness of God. These people are obsessed with peripheral issues while ignoring the most important duty of all: to walk in the love of God, to display mercy to others, and to live with integrity. They are nitpickers, straining gnats and swallowing camels.

These religious zealots sit in the seat of judgment, determined to find everyone's weakness, flaw, or failure so they can exalt themselves over others. This always creates disciples of self-centeredness constantly trying to earn salvation through their works in a do-it-yourself and get-all-the-glory religion.

Let's be honest, most of our lives we have taken our cues from what these pretenders have said. We have allowed them to keep us focused on a list of religious duties, obsessing with peripheral issues, becoming just as narcissistic as they are on their seat of judgment. They have kept us constantly in a cycle of sin-management.

Yet Paul doesn't just warn us of the pretenders but shows us where to keep our focus—the cross!

> *He canceled out every legal violation we had on our record and the old arrest warrant that stood to indict us. He erased it all—our sins, our stained soul—he deleted it all and they cannot be retrieved! Everything we once were in Adam has been placed onto his cross and nailed permanently there as a public display of cancellation (Colossians 2:14).*

It's time to take our eyes off the pretenders around and the pretender within and focus on the cross! His cross stands as a permanent reminder that your record is erased, your stains where sin used to be are gone, and it is all irretrievable. This is the place of the great exchange—Adam's nature has been removed and Christ nature has been embedded. A new DNA has been imparted. Paul said in Galatians 2:19-21:

> *What actually took place is this: I tried keeping rules and working my head off to please God, and it didn't work. So I quit being a "law man" so that I could be God's man. Christ's life showed me how, and enabled me to do it. I identified myself completely with him. Indeed, I have been crucified with Christ. My ego is no longer central. It is no longer important that I appear righteous before you or have your good opinion, and I am no longer driven to impress God. Christ lives in me. The life you see me living is not "mine," but it is lived by faith in the Son of God, who loved me and gave himself for me. I am not going to go back on that. Is it not clear to you that to go back to that*

old rule-keeping, peer-pleasing religion would be an abandonment of everything personal and free in my relationship with God? I refuse to do that, to repudiate God's grace. If a living relationship with God could come by rule-keeping, then Christ died unnecessarily (MSG).

We have liberty in Christ! Paul declared in Colossians 2:16-23:

So why would you allow anyone to judge you because of what you eat or drink, or insist that you keep the feasts, observe new moon celebrations, or the Sabbath? All of these were but a prophetic shadow and the evidence of what would be fulfilled, for the body is now Christ! Don't let anyone disqualify you from your prize! Don't let their pretended sincerity fool you as they deliberately lead you into their initiation of angel worship. For they take pleasure in pretending to be experts of something they know nothing about. Their reasoning is meaningless and comes only from their own opinions. They refuse to take hold of the true source. But we receive directly from him, and his life supplies vitality into every part of his body through the joining ligaments connecting us all as one. He is the divine Head who guides his body and causes it to grow by the supernatural power of God. For you were included in the death of Christ and have died with him to the religious system and powers of this world. Don't retreat back to being bullied by the standards and opinions of religion—for example, their strict requirements, "You can't associate with that person!" or, "Don't eat that!" or, "You can't touch that!" These are the doctrines of men and corrupt customs that are worthless to help you spiritually. For though they may appear to possess the promise of wisdom in their submission to God through the deprivation of their physical bodies, it is actually nothing more than empty rules rooted in religious rituals!

So then what is our responsibility in becoming a carrier of the Presence of God? Jesus said in John 6:29, "This is the only work God wants from you: Believe in the one he has sent" (NLT).

Believe in Christ!

So as we come to a close in this book, my prayer is that you would take the road less traveled into the purity of the gospel. That you would see yourself in Christ as a carrier of the very Presence of God. You in Christ and Christ in you is the way your city is going to experience the glory of God.

I hope that more than pointing out the failures of the current Western expression of Christianity, I want you to inherit keys and direction that can point you to Christ! Christ calls us to Himself, to fathers, and to the family so we can become the sons of glory. God has and always will want to be carried by people, and it is by way of the gospel that this happens effortlessly. I pray you are able to abandon the old way and fully step into the new.

If you are a leader, recognize the dysfunctional models of leadership that were passed down to us and, like David, have one focus—the Presence of Jesus. Give permission for those you lead to come into the fullness of grace and provide an atmosphere where everyone can break their box without the fear of man.

If you find yourselves in a systemic church filled with the dry dead traditions of Western people, in honor, exit that place and find a spiritual father. Get joined to a local kingdom family expression that is endeavoring to make it all about Jesus! You, like David, have been born for this very hour.

As I finished writing the manuscript of the book that you now hold in your hand, I sensed from the Lord a dynamic shift in our ministry. For years I have pointed at the failing model of the Western church in all of its dysfunction. But I know from the Lord that this book is my last letter to the old world.

I will no longer mourn for Saul or point out the flaws of the compromised priesthood or even the traveling prophets. This book is a bridge for years to come for anyone who wants a way out. But I must lay down the sword and tools I have used over the years to "uproot, tear down, destroy, and overthrow." It's now time for me in the grace of God to build and plant for a new world.

Many of you have left that old world behind and have said to yourself, "Now what?" It's time to build something beautiful. With the Presence of God restored back to the center of our lives, we will be granted peace to gather resources for the Solomons who with wisdom and creativity will bring the Kingdom into an age of absolute brilliance.

It's time to release the beauty of Jesus and show the world the beauty of His Kingdom within the church. He is going to change the way we speak and see the Bride. We have mourned for Saul long enough, and it's time to anoint David, learn beauty and beloved identity, and show the world the glory of God.

We all know the system was dysfunctional. I know many were wounded there, but we are not there anymore. His church is beautiful, so it's time to remove the negative speech from our mouth, the complaining, and any critical spirit. We must learn how Abba speaks and how Jesus wants to woo His Bride into her true identity.

It's a new day for the sons of glory to arise and build the tabernacle of David for a new world!

Notes

1. William Martin, "Divorce, drugs, drinking: Billy Graham's children and their absent father," The Washington Post, February 21, 2018, https://www.washingtonpost.com/news/acts-of-faith/wp/2018/02/21/divorce-drugs-drinking-billy-grahams-children-and-their-absent-father.

2. A.W. Tozer, *The Root of the Righteous*, https://awtozer.com/2019/09/24/the-root-of-the-righteous.

3. A.W. Tozer, *The Knowledge of the Holy* (San Francisco: HaperCollins, 1961), 3-4.

4. R. Dennis Cole, *Numbers* (Nashville, TN: B&H Publishing Group, 2000), 99-100.

5. John G. Lake, "How God Gave Me the Ministry of Healing and Sent Me to Africa," https://pdfroom.com/books/john-g-lake-sermons/Pe5xQjDRdnN.

About Mark Casto

Mark Casto is the lead pastor of The Shepherd's Tent. He is the host of The Family Table Podcast featured on the Destiny Image Podcast Network. He and his wife, Destani, live in Covington, Georgia, with their four children, Elijah, Ezekiel, Elliana, and Eden. To say hi or to connect with more of Mark's resources, go to: **http://markcasto.co.**

Journal

YOUR Prophetic COMMUNITY

Are you passionate about hearing God's voice, walking with Jesus, and experiencing the power of the Holy Spirit?

Destiny Image is a community of believers with a passion for equipping and encouraging you to live the prophetic, supernatural life you were created for!

We offer a fresh helping of practical articles, dynamic podcasts, and powerful videos from respected, Spirit-empowered, Christian leaders to fuel the holy fire within you.